THE MAGIC OF
CHRISTMAS

THE MAGIC OF
CHRISTMAS

FACTS BEHIND THE MYTHS AND
MAGIC OF CHRISTMAS

PATRICK HARDING

metro

Published by Metro Publishing Ltd, 3 Bramber Court,
2 Bramber Road, London W14 9PB, England

First published in hardback in 2004

ISBN 1 84358 124 8

British Library Cataloguing-in-Publication Data: A catalogue record for
this book is available from the British Library.

Design by www.envydesign.co.uk

Printed and bound in Great Britain by CPD (Wales)

1 3 5 7 9 10 8 6 4 2

Pictures reproduced by kind permission of the
Mary Evans Picture Library
Line drawings of holly and mistletoe © Jean Binney

Papers used by Metro Publishing Ltd are natural, recyclable
products made from wood grown in sustainable forests.
The manufacturing processes conform to the environmental
regulations of the country of origin.

Every attempt has been made to contact the relevant
copyright-holders, but some were unobtainable. We would
be grateful if the appropriate people could contact us

DEDICATION

I dedicate this book to my father-in-law,
Jack Binney — a man every bit as generous
as Father Christmas.

CONTENTS

CHRISTMAS CUSTOMS

THE GOOSE IS GETTING FAT

OTHER CHRISTMAS QUIRKS AND QUERIES

ACKNOWLEDGEMENTS

O ver the years, many people have helped me with this book. This is particularly true where those who, having attended one of my talks on Christmas customs, have given me their own stories or sent me newspaper cuttings to add to my collection. To all those people, a big thank you.

Among those who have helped check particular sections for me are Twm Elias, Colin Ennis, James Forster, Gordon Garrity, David Harding, Jean Harding, Phil Healy, Rob and Helen Kelly, Mary Sharrock, Trev Sullivan, Derek Whiteley and Rev Peter Williams.

The following organisations provided helpful information: Archives of Cultural Tradition at the University of Sheffield, Chesterfield Museum, Norwich Tourist Office, York Tourist Office and The Vegetarian Society. Mayfield Computers, Sheffield sorted out all my technology problems and Ken Chung provided neat copy for the publishers.

My niece, Charlotte Harding, undertook the

mammoth task of checking the whole manuscript. This was carried out quickly and efficiently and I am very grateful for her help.

Jean Binney (my long-suffering wife) not only provided original pen and ink pictures for the book but read over the initial drafts and kept me well fed and watered as I laboured in my study.

THE ONES I USED TO KNOW

Once Upon a Time at Christmas

In the 21st century, Christmas ('Christ's Mass') is a worldwide time of celebration and commercial exploitation shared not only by millions of Christians but by people of other faiths and those of no faith in particular. For most people, including many Christians, any religious significance has become buried under the trappings of an age far removed from that of 2,000 years ago. Most British children consider Santa Claus to be the key figure associated with 25 December. The average person has a limited understanding of the Nativity story and of the origins of our Christmas customs, something this book hopes to rectify.

For the past ten years, I have presented talks about Christmas and its customs to a wide range of groups and societies including women's institutes, church groups, university classes and pagan federations. Only rarely do I find people in the audience whose knowledge of the Nativity has not been clouded by the views of parents, teachers or the Church. The result is a nation split between those with a dogmatic belief in 'facts' and those, as portrayed by the character of Charles Ryder in *Brideshead Revisited*, who remain scornful of those believing in 'Christmas and the star and the three kings and the ox and the ass'.

'What animals,' I ask at my talks, 'are mentioned in the Gospels as being present at the birth of Jesus?' Ox and ass, comes the reply, along with donkeys and the odd camel, together with lots of sheep. The last-named may have been part of the watched-over flocks of the Gospel account (goats are much more common in the Middle East) but of the ox, ass, donkey and camel there is no word. As a starting point, it is important to see exactly what the Gospel accounts *do* tell us of the events surrounding the Nativity. The following extracts are taken from the King James version of the Bible:

> Now when Jesus was born in Bethlehem of Judaea in the days of Herod the king, behold, there came wise men from the east to Jerusalem, Saying where is he that is born King of the Jews? for we have seen his star in the east, and are come to worship him. When Herod the king had heard these things, he was troubled, and all Jerusalem with him. And when he had gathered all the chief

priests and scribes of the people together, he demanded of them where Christ should be born. And they said unto him in Bethlehem of Judaea: for thus it is written by the prophet, And thou Bethlehem, in the land of Juda, art not the least among the princes of Juda: for out of thee shall come a Governor, that shall rule my people Israel. Then Herod, when he had privily called the wise men, inquired of them diligently what time the star appeared. And he sent them to Bethlehem, and said, Go and search diligently for the young child; and when you have found him, bring me word again, that I may come and worship him also. When they had heard the king they departed; and lo, the star which they saw in the east, went before them, till it came and stood over where the young child was. When they saw the star, they rejoiced with exceeding great joy.

And when they were come into the house, they saw the young child with Mary his mother, and fell down, and worshipped him: and when they had opened their treasures, they presented unto him gifts; gold, and frankincense, and myrrh. And being warned of God in a dream that they should not return to Herod, they departed into their own country another way. Then Herod, when he saw that he was mocked of the wise men, was exceeding wroth, and sent forth, and slew all the children that were in Bethlehem, and in all the coasts thereof, from two years old and under, according to the time which he had diligently inquired of the wise men.

(Matthew 2: 1–12,16)

So Jesus was born in Bethlehem during the reign of King Herod and was brought presents by wise men from the east (notice there is no mention of three wise men, only three presents) who were guided by a special star. As we shall see later, the presence of Herod and the star are two important clues in the determination of exactly when Jesus was born.

Luke records the same event in Chapter 2, Verses 1–16:

And it came to pass in those days, that there went out a decree from Caesar Augustus, that all the world should be taxed. (And this taxing was first made when Cyrenius was governor of Syria.) And all went to be taxed, every one into his own city. And Joseph also went up from Galilee, out of the city of Nazareth, into Judaea, unto the city of David, which is called Bethlehem; (because he was of the house and lineage of David) to be taxed with Mary his espoused wife, being great with child. And so it was, that, while they were there, the days were accomplished that she should be delivered. And she brought forth her firstborn son, and wrapped him in swaddling clothes, and laid him in a manger; because there was no room for them in the inn. And there were in the same country shepherds abiding in the field, keeping watch over their flock by night. And, lo, the angel of the Lord came upon them, and the glory of the Lord shone round about them: and they were sore afraid.

And the angel said unto them, Fear not: for, behold, I bring you tidings of great joy, which shall be to all people. For unto you is born this day in the city of David a Saviour, which is Christ the Lord. And this shall be a sign unto you; Ye shall find the babe wrapped in swaddling clothes, lying in a manger. And suddenly there was with the angel a multitude of the heavenly host praising God, and saying, Glory to God in the highest, and on earth peace, good will toward men. And it came to pass, as the angels were gone away from them into heaven, the shepherds said one to another, Let us now go even unto Bethlehem, and see the thing which has come to pass, which the Lord hath made known unto us. And they came with haste, and found Mary, and Joseph, and the babe lying in a manger.

Luke's account confirms Bethlehem as the birth place, giving us the picture of a town full of people conforming with the taxation order made by the

Roman Emperor, Caesar Augustus. There being no room at the inn, Jesus was placed in a manger where, shortly afterwards, he was visited by shepherds, who had been told of the Nativity by an angel.

The Gospels of Mark and John only record the divine or spiritual birth of Jesus:

> And it came to pass in those days, that Jesus came from Nazareth of Galilee, and was baptised of John in Jordan. And straightway coming up out of the water, he saw the heavens opened, and the Spirit like a dove descending upon him: And there came a voice from heaven, saying, Thou art my beloved Son, in whom I am well pleased.
>
> (Mark 1: 9 –11)

> The next day John seeth Jesus coming unto him, and saith, Behold the Lamb of God, which taketh away the sin of the world. This is he of whom I said, After me cometh a man which is preferred before me: for he was before me. And I knew him not: but that he should be made manifest to Israel, therefore am I come baptising with water. And John bare record, saying, I saw the Spirit descending from heaven like a dove, and it abode upon him.
>
> (John 29: 29 –34)

Both of these accounts record the baptism of the adult

Jesus by John in what was probably the Jordan river or one of its tributaries. Recent excavations in Jordan have unearthed the possible baptism site; another is situated across the Jordan Valley in the West Bank.

None of the Gospel accounts mentions that the birth took place in a stable. This idea comes from the

THE INNS ARE FULL

Western association of mangers with farms and especially stables. The definition of a manger is a trough filled with straw from which animals feed. Stone mangers are still found in some of the older houses belonging to peasant stock in the Middle East. Two thousand years ago few animals were provided with a separate stable, but spent the night on the earth floor of the 'living room' (complete with a manger and its provisions) while their owners slept above on a sort of mezzanine level. One commentator, Roger Highfield, pointed out that this would not only provide warmth, from the animals, but also maximise the animals' security against robbers and predators.

Most current-day Nativity plays also contain a reference to Mary and Joseph being turned away from an inn or boarding house (Luke 2: 7). The Ancient Greek word used by Luke was *kataluma* and, like many words, it has more than one meaning. One of these is indeed 'inn', but other meanings include 'house' and 'guest room'. Theologians believe that Joseph and Mary are much

BY THE END OF THE 3RD CENTURY THE CHURCH DECIDED THAT, THOUGH JESUS HAD INDEED BEEN BORN DIVINE, IT WAS IN THE FORM OF A MAN, AND IT BECAME CUSTOMARY TO CELEBRATE HIS BIRTH. BY THEN THE BIRTH DATE HAD BEEN LONG FORGOTTEN ...

more likely to have been put up by family friends in their home town than to have sought accommodation at an inn. Matthew mentions that the wise men 'come into the house'. If the guest room of their friends was already full (no room in the 'inn') then Mary and Joseph would have stayed in the living room, hence the proximity of a manger in which to lay the new born child. The presence of animals at the birth would depend on whether this took place at night or not. The widely held belief that the birth occurred at midnight is not supported by the Gospels or other contemporary accounts of the event.

These are the particulars of the story; so when did the birth actually happen?

When was Jesus Born?

The answer to this question seems obvious, especially so soon after the year 2000 celebrations, but it's more complex than it looks.

The first problem is that early Christians did not celebrate Christmas. They believed in the imminent return of Jesus (in the form of a second coming) and also considered that his divine birth, when the spirit of God descended into him while he was being baptised, was much more important than his physical birth. Of the four Gospel accounts of the life of Jesus, neither Mark nor John has anything to say about the birth of the infant Christ; their first chapters concentrate on his much later baptism.

Even as late as AD 245, Christian Church leaders considered it a sin to celebrate the birthday of Jesus, seeing this as comparable to celebrating the birthday of a mere mortal such as an emperor. By the end of the 3rd century the Church decided that, though Jesus had indeed been born divine, it was in the form of a man, and it became customary to celebrate his birth. By then the birth date had been long forgotten and different branches of the Church chose different occasions on which to honour the event. These included several dates in January and others in March, April and September, but 25 December was not one of them.

The more easterly Christians, based in Alexandria, chose 6 January. This was the date of the supposedly virgin birth of the Greek god Dionysus, renowned for revealing himself as a god by turning water into wine, an act known as an epiphany. To eastern Christians, 6 January was associated with the visit of the Magi (wise men), shortly after the birth of Jesus and the manifestation of his divine nature (Epiphany). This day was also remembered as the one on which, many years later, Jesus was baptised. So the eastern Church combined the festival of Christ's birth and epiphany with that of his baptism, neatly sidestepping any arguments about celebrating the physical birth of Christ. To this day Christmas is still celebrated on 6 January in Armenia, the first nation to embrace Christianity.

Meanwhile, the western branch of the Christian Church, based in Rome, attached more significance to the visit of the Magi on 6 January and commemorated it as the Epiphany. They chose to celebrate Christ's baptism on the Sunday after Epiphany and Christ's nativity during the slightly earlier festival of Christmas. Opinions differ as to exactly when 25 December became their date for Christmas but it was probably early in the 4th century (see page 42).

Two more problems remain: first, 25 December is only Jesus's 'official' birthday and, second, there is considerable debate concerning attempts to determine the precise *year* of the birth.

But In Which Year?

It is not easy to work out the exact year in which Jesus was born. This is due to an age-old dilemma: try constructing a calendar when no one can agree on the precise length of a year. *The Calendar*, a fascinating book by David Duncan, details many of the difficulties that have beset calendar makers through the ages.

A major problem is that an easy-to-observe-and-measure *lunar* year of 354 days (on which the Islamic calendar year is based), consisting of 12 lunar months, each of 29.5 days, is significantly shorter than a *solar* year. A solar year (just over 365 days) is the length of time taken for the Earth to orbit the sun, the process that drives the seasons. Precise measurement of this has proved difficult, particularly when it was believed that the sun went round the Earth ...

Estimating the dates of important festivals, like the winter solstice (the shortest day), was made harder still by the fact that the Earth travels round the sun in an asymmetrical orbit.

Our current calendar combines a number of previous attempts, beginning with the one said to have been set up by Romulus in 735 BC, at the founding of Rome. The first year of this calendar was known as 1 AUC (*ab urbe condita*, 'from the founding of the city'). Years were based on only ten months (most of which were slightly longer than a lunar month). The first four months were given descriptive names and the year started in Martis, now March, named after the god of war. The final six months were named after the Latin for fifth, sixth, etc. Thus the last (tenth) month became December. In total, the year lasted for just 304 days. Later, the poet Ovid pointed out that this was rather closer to the human gestation period than to the length of a seasonal year. Celebrations, festivals and important agricultural practices such as sowing times were all noted on the calendar (having previously been determined by the positions of the sun and moon) but, based on a year of just 304 days, these quickly fell out of synch with the seasons.

Some years later, two extra months (our current January and February) were added to the *end* of each year. Together with other adjustments this took the Roman calendar year to just one day longer than the lunar year – a total of 355 days (the Romans believed that even numbers were unlucky). Even this calendar required the addition of extra days (and occasionally months) to maintain its alignment with the seasons.

Julius Caesar sought to rectify this seasonal drift by

ordering that there be a total of 445 days in the year 46 BC; little wonder it became known as the year of confusion. Caesar then instigated a reformed year of some 365¼ days (2000 years after the Ancient Egyptians had calculated this to be the length of the solar year). The ten days added to the old Roman 355-day calendar were distributed throughout the 12 months. Conveniently, this resulted in alternating 31-day (starting with January) and 30-day months. February, however, only had 30 days every fourth year (called a leap year) and 29 days in other years. Having an extra day every four years got round the problem of having a year of 365¼ days.

The year of 45 BC (709 AUC) not only adhered to the Julian calendar (as it is now known) but began not in March, but on 1 January. The first day of each month was by then known as kalends, and this name was also given to the New Year festival on 1 January. It's likely that this date resulted from the Roman custom of beginning a year with a new moon, coupled with the practice of starting a year after the midwinter solstice. The year 708 AUC ended on 30 December and a new moon appeared on the following day (1 January 709).

Unfortunately, after Julius Caesar's death, leap years were inserted every three, rather than every four, years. This mistake was rectified under the Emperor Augustus Caesar by not adding extra days in what should have been leap years between 8 BC and AD 8. Jesus was probably born during this period of correction.

The Roman Senate renamed the year's eighth month

in honour of Augustus, and upset the alternation of 30/31 days by announcing that there were to be 31 days in this month (it would be equal to the previous month, which had been renamed to honour Julius). This would have resulted in three 31-day months in a row, a dilemma avoided by switching the lengths of the four final months of the year. Unfortunately, this destroyed the alternating 30/31 pattern in both July/August and December/January. The extra day in August was compensated for by reducing the already short month of February to only 28 days, with 29 in a leap year.

By the time of the birth of Jesus the calendar was based on a fairly accurate estimation of the solar year. It overestimated the year by just 11 minutes and 14 seconds, a great improvement on earlier Roman calendars. However, the fact that the true solar year was shorter than the calendar year by about one day every 128 years meant that over the centuries the calendar year drifted further from the solar year. Many hundreds of years later this led to another calendar adjustment. Some of the effects of this on Christmas and its customs are discussed on page 234.

The dates mentioned, for example AD 8, were not at the time known under this notation. Surprisingly, the AD numbering system, far from pinpointing the Nativity year, only added to the difficulty in determining the exact year of Christ's birth.

The AD system, initiated in the 6th century, was part of a drive by the western branch of the Christian Church in Rome to calculate future dates for the movable feast of

Easter (unlike Christmas which had been fixed on 25 December). Previously, the Church in Rome had been forced to rely on astrological and other calculations made by the Christian Church in Alexandria.

The man chosen by Pope John I to predict the future dates of Easter was the abbot Dionysius Exiguus, who because of his short stature is now commonly referred to as 'Little Dennis'. He came up with a method of predicting future dates for Easter Sunday based on rules laid down at an important meeting of bishops that had been held some 200 years earlier.

The meeting was organised by the emperor Constantine at Nicaea, some 80 miles from Constantinople, now Istanbul. The bishops agreed that Easter should be celebrated on the first Sunday following the first full moon after the spring equinox, unless the resulting day coincided with the start of the Jewish Passover festival, in which case it was moved to the following Sunday.

Dionysius had to be able to predict the precise dates of full moons for years ahead (something he did with the help of the 19-year cycle of lunar months that links the lunar and solar year) and he also needed to know the exact date of the spring equinox. Partly because of the effect of the extra day in February during a leap year, this is not always on 21 March. Fortunately for the abbot, the Niccacan conference had decided that 21 March would be the official Church date for the equinox. (In the year 2000 Easter Sunday was celebrated on 23 April, the latest Easter date for almost 60 years as the first full moon after 21 March was not until 18 April.)

Dionysius produced tables calculating the date of Easter for the following 96 years and added an innovation in that he changed the base date used to number these years. At the time the Roman calendar no longer originated with the founding of Rome but took as its year 1 the beginning of the reign of the emperor Diocletian. In the year 247 *anni Diocletiani* the abbot Dionysius recorded his dislike for a system that honoured an emperor who had created the 'Era of Martyrs' by persecuting Christians. Instead, Dionysius used a dating system based on 'the years from the incarnation of our Lord' in the preparation of his Easter tables.

Dionysius calculated that Jesus had been born 531 years earlier, in what he called year 1 (at the time, zero was not a mathematical entity in the West) and his tables were headed *anno Domini nostri Jesu Christi* 532 – 627. The notation, later shortened to *anno Domini*, gives us the AD prefix. The change to the new numbering system was neither rapid nor inclusive and Egyptian (Coptic) Christians still use *anni Diocletiani*. Their year 1716 corresponded to our year 2000. The BC notation, numbering the years before the birth of Christ, first appeared in the 17th century.

We should now be in a position to name the year of Christ's birth, but only if the calculations of Dionysius, made over 500 years after the event, are accurate. Sadly, this seems unlikely. Dionysius (or someone else if he was not the original calculator) is believed to have determined the base date for the AD system by totalling the years reigned by all the Roman emperors from the time of the birth of Jesus to the then present time. Unfortunately, the four-year rule of the emperor Octavian was overlooked and not included in the calculations.

This would put the year of the birth closer to 4 BC and leave us wondering whether other smaller errors in the calculation might have further distorted the true time span since the Nativity. It certainly looks as though the recent millennium celebrations were a number of years too late. If we cannot rely precisely on Dionysius and the AD system, what clues as to the year and season of the Nativity can we obtain from the Bible?

IT LOOKS AS THOUGH THE RECENT MILLENNIUM CELEBRATIONS WERE A NUMBER OF YEARS TOO LATE. IF WE CANNOT RELY PRECISELY ON DIONYSIUS AND THE AD SYSTEM, WHAT CLUES AS TO THE YEAR AND SEASON OF THE NATIVITY CAN WE OBTAIN FROM THE BIBLE?

What do the Gospels and the Stars Say?

The Gospel stories of the Nativity contain a number of clues to a possible year of Jesus's birth. Perhaps the most significant of these is the reference to a star in the east that was seen by the Magi (see the Matthew extract, page 12). Theologians take Matthew's account as a fulfilment of the Old Testament prophecy 'there shall come a star out of Jacob, and a sceptre shall rise out of Israel' (Numbers 24: 17).

Again the imprecise art of translation may have played its part. The original Greek word *Magi* (singular *Magus*) is translated in the King James version of the Bible as 'wise men', while the New English Bible uses 'astrologers' as a more meaningful translation. Babylon was an important early centre for astrological study, but

THE ORIGINAL GREEK WORD MAGI IS TRANSLATED IN THE KING JAMES VERSION OF THE BIBLE AS 'WISE MEN', WHILE THE NEW ENGLISH BIBLE USES 'ASTROLOGERS' AS A MORE MEANINGFUL TRANSLATION.

by the time of the birth of Jesus many Magi had moved from Babylon and settled in neighbouring regions. The ruins of Babylon have been found some 55 miles south of Baghdad in what is now Iraq. It is probable that the Magi referred to in the Bible travelled to Bethlehem from what today would be part of either Iran or Saudi Arabia.

Recently, astronomers worked out the exact date in 1890 when Van Gogh painted *White House at Night*, a picture that depicts a house at twilight under a prominent yellow star. Could a similar analysis of the 2000-year-old positions of the planets, constellations and comets (as viewed from the Middle East) throw light on the biblical 'star' and help to pinpoint the date of its sighting? Astronomers have carried out such research, but their results have resulted in conflicting claims as to what could have been described as a 'star in the east' and when it would have been visible in the night sky.

It is a popular belief, and one portrayed in many paintings and Christmas card images, that the 'star' was a comet. As such, one obvious contender is the

THE ADORATION OF THE MAGI

well-known Halley's comet. Astronomers have calculated that this would have been visible in 12 BC but, even allowing for the miscalculations of the AD numbering system, this is too early to have coincided with the Nativity. Some years later (in 5 BC) Chinese astronomers recorded sightings of a different comet that was visible for over two months. Professor Humphreys of Cambridge University believes that this could have been the biblical 'star'. If so, it indicates that the Nativity occurred in April/May of the year 5 BC.

Others rule out such an obvious event as the sighting of a comet, arguing that this would have been recorded by more than just one of the Apostles. They also consider that a comet would have been noticed by Herod's court (according to Matthew this was not the case). As it happens, astrology was a practice forbidden to the Jews of the time (the planets were deemed to be pagan gods), so Herod could have learnt about less obvious astronomical features from the visiting Magi (astrologers).

Research indicates that the Magi of the time were very interested in interpreting the movements of the planets and the signs of the zodiac. If this is so, an event that occurred three times in the year 7 BC (and was first analysed in 1603 by the German astronomer Johannes Kepler) would have been much more significant to the Magi than a comet. The event is known as a triple conjunction, which, in 7 BC, involved the apparent closeness of the planets Jupiter and Saturn set against the stars composing the constellation of Pisces.

Jupiter was the king of the gods, so astrologers would take the presence of that planet as pertaining to a king, whilst Saturn represented justice and the land of Palestine. Many scholars believe that Pisces was the sign of the zodiac that represented the Jews, hence the unusual conjunction was taken to forecast the coming of a Jewish Messiah. Working with star maps representing the heavens in the year 7 BC, researchers have calculated that the triple conjunction first occurred in May, then again in September/October and finally in November/December.

While it's tempting to jump to the December conjunction as fitting with our idea of the season of the Nativity, Luke's reference to 'shepherds keeping watch over their flock' points to the spring (the lambing season) or autumn (when the sheep were rounded up). David Hughes of Sheffield University has suggested that the Magi may have travelled during the second conjunction, when the hot summer was over, thus suggesting an autumn birth; a theory upheld by John the Baptist's supposed birth in late March. John was said to precede Jesus by six months. Today we celebrate St John's day on 24 June, some six months before the generally accepted Christmas date of 25 December.

Others scholars think that the triple conjunctions of 7 BC plus another of Mars, Jupiter and Saturn in 6 BC and the comet observed in 5 BC were all signs that preceded the birth in 5 BC. A further possibility emerges from the work of the American astronomer Michael Molnar. He is intrigued by an early Roman coin depicting a star over a ram, and argues that in those days Aries (the ram), and not Pisces, was symbolic of the land of Judea. As such a 'star' in the constellation of Aries would have been most significant. He has shown that in both March and April 6 BC the planet Jupiter was eclipsed 'in the east' in Aries. Recently, Molnar has come across details of this in a book written by Maternus in AD 334. Maternus commented that the event signified the birth of a divine king but did not mention that this had been Jesus, possibly because early Christians were loath to use the pagan practice of astrology to support the Nativity story.

In addition to the missing four years in the calculation of the AD calendar (see page 27), it is very unlikely that Jesus was born later than 4 BC because this is now thought to be when King Herod died. The details of Herod's death are scant but it is believed to have occurred within a few days of an eclipse of the moon. Together with other evidence relating to when his son succeeded him, the eclipse that would have been visible from Palestine on 13 March, 4 BC, would seem to be the one coinciding with Herod's death. That the birth of Jesus was some years before Herod's death is suggested by Matthew's account:

> Then Herod ... slew all the children that were in Bethlehem, and in all the coasts thereof, from two years old and under, according to the time which he had diligently inquired of the wise men.
> (Matthew 2: 16)

In the year 2000 it was reported that a mass grave dating from the time of Herod had been excavated at a site near Bethlehem. All the bones were of infants, 70 per cent being male. If the Bible story is accurate (and it is commemorated on 28 December as Holy Innocents' Day) we can conclude that Jesus was born about two years before Herod's death in 4 BC, once again bringing us back to around 6 or 7 BC.

An eclipse of the moon has also helped scholars such as Colin Humphreys to determine the likely date of the Crucifixion. Contemporary accounts talk of the Friday close to the Jewish Passover, while biblical references include Acts 2: 20, 'The sun shall be turned into darkness, and the moon into blood.' This reddish colour occurs during a lunar eclipse (and was clearly seen in parts of Britain during a total eclipse of the moon on 9 January 2001). Such an eclipse, visible in the Middle East during the reign of Pontius Pilate, occurred on Friday 3 April AD 33. Unfortunately, we don't know how old Jesus was when he died so we cannot calculate his birth year by working backwards from AD 33. References to Jesus being 33 when he died are based on the false assumption that the AD system is correct.

Luke's account (page 14) tells us that Mary and Joseph travelled to Bethlehem in order to be taxed under orders from Caesar Augustus, at a time when Cyrenius was governor of Syria. Sadly, this information does little to help us in our search, as the account appears to be inaccurate. Historians have found evidence of a census ordered by Augustus in 7 or 8 BC, but this appears to have only been for Roman citizens. The fact that censuses took many years to complete makes the taxation issue even less useful in the hunt for the year in question. More confusingly, other evidence shows that Cyrenius did not become governor of Syria until AD 6.

Whatever the exact date of the Nativity, most scholars believe it to have been no later than some time in the year 4 BC and probably no earlier than 7 BC. What is almost certain is that 1 January 2000 was not 2000 years after the birth of Christ; such a celebration should have been held some six or seven years earlier. Even if the AD calculations of Dionysius had been correct, mathematicians have pointed out that the new millennium should have started on 1 January 2001 – so much for all the hype at the end of 1999.

So the commonly accepted *year* of Christ's birth is probably six to seven years too late. As for 25 December, this is comparable to the Queen's official birthday and is very unlikely to be the actual birth date of Christ. So why did the western branch of the Christian Church choose to celebrate Christmas on 25 December?

So Why Move the Feast to 25 December?

During the 3rd century, many Christians believed that the incarnation (conception) of Christ had occurred at the spring equinox, then reckoned to be on 25 March. Nine months on meant a Nativity date of 25

December, the date later chosen by the Church based in Rome on which to celebrate Christmas. There was no evidence (then or now) that this actually was the day on which Jesus had been born, so why was it chosen? The reason appears to have been a pragmatic one – a 25 December Christmas slotted neatly into the Roman calendar in the midst of a host of other celebrations. As a result those celebrating Christmas remained relatively inconspicuous and also missed little of the fun of more traditional celebrations as Christmas absorbed many customs from these more long-standing festivals.

Long before the birth of the Roman Empire, people from the Middle East and more northern parts of Europe celebrated the annual renewal of the sun's strength as part of their midwinter festivals. In the intriguingly titled book 4000 *Years of Christmas*, many present-day Christmas customs are traced to Mesopotamia (modern-day Iraq) and its year-end celebrations associated with the renewal of the sun's strength following the winter solstice. Thousands of years before the birth of Christ these festivities included the giving of presents, the lighting of fires and a period of about 12 days for 'making merry'.

The Mesopotamians believed that their chief god Marduk had routed 'the monsters of chaos' and so built an orderly world. This order ran down by the end of the year and had to be renewed during the Zagmuk festival. Effigies of Marduck's opponents were burnt on bonfires and people exchanged gifts. Their king was supposed to die at the end of the year so that he could descend into the underworld and help Marduck do battle to restore order. Instead a mock king (possibly a criminal) was chosen to rule for the 12 days, but at the end of the festival he was slain in place of the true king.

In a similar festival (Sacaea) celebrated by the Persians, masters and slaves changed places and in each household a slave became the temporary head. This was part of the general relaxing of rules as the old year died. Other accounts of gods conquering chaos and evil are found in the stories of Ancient Greece where Zeus replaced Marduck and defeated Kronos and the Titans in his battles to restore order.

To the Romans the good god of long ago was epitomised by Saturn, the god of sowing and husbandry, who was said to have brought order to Italy. Among his many virtues Saturn was said to have taught the people how to till the ground and live in peace with each other, all being considered equal. The good times under Saturn were remembered by the Romans in their annual festival of Saturnalia (and prior to Constantine's change in AD 321, by having Saturn's Day – Saturday – as a day of rest and worship). As a result of various calendar changes the exact dates of Saturnalia altered during the Roman era but the festival is usually regarded as having lasted from 17 December to 24 December.

Many elements of the Saturnalia festival had their roots in older celebrations. Several customs associated with the Christmas festival were clearly borrowed from

Saturnalia, which would have been well known to these early Christians. Like the Zagmuk festival, Saturnalia had its darker side, though here the sacrifices were more likely to have been animal, rather than human. The freemen of Rome drew lots to elect a mock king (a further similarity with the more ancient festival of Zagmuk) who then issued silly and playful commands as part of the general merry making. Unlike his predecessors the mock king escaped being sacrificed at the end of his term in office.

Saturnalia was a time of overeating (*saturnus* means plenty) and general boisterousness, but it was also when people visited friends and gave them gifts to wish them good luck for the coming year. These gifts were known as *strenae* and were originally fruits but later included cakes among other things. In addition, homes were decorated with the branches of evergreen trees and plenty of lamps and candles. Such customs were also part of the Roman New Year festival of Kalends that closely followed on from Saturnalia. Likewise, the intermingling of Christmas and New Year customs has become commonplace.

THERE WAS A MORE RELAXED DRESS CODE WHEN MEN PUT ON ANIMAL SKINS OR WOMEN'S CLOTHES AND SOME WOMEN DRESSED AS MEN. IT WAS ALSO A TIME FOR GREATER SEXUAL FREEDOM, THE LATTER NO DOUBT STIMULATED BY AN EXCESSIVE CONSUMPTION OF ALCOHOL. THE 'GOINGS ON' AT CHRISTMAS PARTIES IN THE 21ST CENTURY PALE BY COMPARISON.

It is descriptions of the lighter side of the Saturnalia celebrations that earlier writers have passed on to us.

These include the closure of businesses and schools and the relaxing of the strict rules governing the behaviour of slaves, to the extent that masters changed places with their servants and even waited on them at table. This reflects the teachings of Saturn (that all men were considered equal) at a time when slavery was unheard of. To this day officers in the British forces serve a special Christmas meal to the lower ranks. Similar temporary changes of rank occur at many workplace Christmas parties.

Other Saturnalia customs included gambling, something that was forbidden to most peoples at all other times. There was also a more relaxed dress code, when men put on animal skins or women's clothes and some women dressed as men. It was also a time for wearing hats, and a licence for greater sexual freedom, the latter no doubt stimulated by an excessive consumption of alcohol. The 'goings on' at Christmas parties in the 21st century pale by comparison.

Perhaps the most important festival of the Christmas season throughout northern Europe and the Middle East was that linked to the shortest day (the winter solstice). According to our current (Gregorian) calendar the winter solstice normally falls on either 21 December or 22 December. Due to the asymmetrical orbit of the earth round the sun, the latest sunrise time in Britain occurs not on the winter solstice but a few days later. The Romans calculated that 25 December (in their Julian calendar) represented the sun at its lowest ebb.

So it was that 25 December, the day after the end of Saturnalia, was the most important day of the year for the many Roman followers of Mithraism, an ancient religion that spread from Persia (Iran). Mithraism, based on the worship of the sun god Mithra (also known as Mithras) was, by the 3rd century AD, a serious rival to the spread of Christianity in the Roman Empire. Aurelian, who ruled the Roman Empire from AD 270 to 275, even declared that Mithra, not the Senate, had made him emperor. In AD 274 he proclaimed that 25 December was to be the date for observing the birthday of the sun. Many wealthy Romans erected altars to Mithras and some of these have been found at Roman sites in Britain.

The date from which days began lengthening was considered to be 25 December, and it was celebrated as the rebirth or resurrection (from its winter death) of 'the unconquered sun'. The Latin word 'natalis', meaning birthday (source of the English word 'Nativity' and the French word 'Noel'), was originally indicative of the birth of the sun on 25 December. The book *The Golden Bough*, by J. G. Frazer, recounts that devout followers of Mithraism had greeted the dawn of the 25th with the cry 'The Virgin has brought forth! The light is waxing!' The newborn sun was even represented by the image of an infant.

The 4th-century Roman emperor Constantine, who did more than any other figure (apart from his mother Helena) to help Christianity become the official religion of the Roman Empire, had previously flirted with Mithraism. Coins produced during the early part of his reign depicted the unconquered sun *Sol Invictus*. An early Roman term for Jesus was *Sol Justitiae* and he was often portrayed in a form remarkably similar to that of the sun god.

Frazer argued that the Christian Church chose 25 December as the date for Christmas in order to facilitate a transfer from a praise of the sun to that of devotion to the 'Sun (son) of Righteousness'. Celebrations to the sun included the ritual lighting of fires, candles and lamps in a belief that this helped the sun to regain its energy. Candles, lights and fires later became associated with the Christmas festival.

Now a brief excursion into Roman history. By the 4th century, the Roman Empire was far removed from its earlier glory-days. It was divided by war. Thus Diocletian, who ruled from AD 284 to 305, was only emperor of part of the area after the year 286. From the year 293 no fewer than four men controlled the empire. Part of Diocletian's infighting included the brutal treatment of Christians, creating what is now called the 'Era of Martyrs'.

A major turning point for his successor, Constantine (who ruled from AD 305 to 336, the last 12 years as sole ruler of the empire), was his decisive victory over Maxentius at the battle of Milvian Bridge in 312. According to early accounts, Constantine saw a vision on the eve of the battle in the form of a cross of light above the sun, emblazoned with the words *en touto nika* – 'in this conquer'. Later, he is said to have dreamed that he heard a voice promising that victory would be his if he placed the sign of the cross on the shields and standards of his soldiers.

In the well-researched book *The Quest for the True Cross*, it is suggested that the sign Constantine duly inscribed was not a simple cross but a form of the Christian symbol known as the Chi-Rho. This was an intertwining of the first two letters of *Christos*, depicted in Greek as X and P. Fortunately for Constantine, whose army would have been made up of soldiers of many different faiths, the inscription bore a striking resemblance to the *tropaeum* symbol used to reflect Roman victories. It was also similar to a cross-like symbol (like a swastika) sacred to the followers of Mithraism.

In the following year Constantine announced that Christianity would enjoy the same rights as cults such as Mithraism, but he rather hedged his bets and only embraced Christianity exclusively on his deathbed. His mother Helena was the driving force behind his support for Christianity that resulted, among other things, in a move of the holy day from Saturday to Sunday. In calling the conference of bishops at Nicaea in AD 325, Constantine laid the ground rules for forecasting those future dates of Easter and, as mentioned on page 25, the conference was instrumental in the later introduction of the AD dating system.

Constantine also paved the way for the move by the Church in Rome (through Pope Julius 1 in AD 352) to a fixed date of 25 December for the Nativity celebration.

One of the earliest mentions of this is in the Roman calendar for the year 354. Later, in the year 380, the emperor Theodosius allowed Christianity to be the Roman Empire's one and only state religion.

A Christmas Calendar

These days many shops begin to market Christmas goods from as early as September, but the main activity before December used to be the making of the Christmas pudding. This is traditionally made on the last Sunday before Advent, on what is still referred to as Stir-Up Sunday.

The formal lead-up to Christmas is the period of Advent, a time of preparation before celebrating the birth of Christ. In the 5th century it began on 11 November (St Martin's Day) and took the form of a six-week fast leading up to Christmas. During the 6th century, Advent was reduced to its current length and later the fasting was dropped. Advent now runs from the fourth Sunday before Christmas Day until 24 December. Historically it was a period of quiet and contemplation prior to Christmas, but this is rarely the case nowadays with visits to overcrowded shops for the purchase of presents, trees, decorations and other seasonal fare.

On each of the four Sundays in Advent special candles are lit in churches. Advent candles were also once common as a pre-Christmas house decoration (the Advent wreath) and more information on this is included in the section on candles on pages 169 and 170. The Advent Calendar is a more recent British custom having been imported from Germany in the 20th century. Traditionally these have scenes relating to the Nativity concealed behind 'windows' labelled from 1 to 24 December. In 2002 the first day of Advent is Sunday 1 December, but in many years Advent does not begin on 1 December; it depends on the date of the Sunday.

Modern Advent calendars have become less religious. A piece of chocolate is often concealed behind each window (quite the antithesis of the original Advent fast), as if preparing children for the overeating that will follow. There is now also often a window for 25 December though this is not strictly part of Advent. The subject matter of the best-selling Advent calendars has also strayed from the Nativity theme. It is ironic that December 2001 witnessed huge sales of Harry Potter Advent calendars, an interesting mix of religion and the darker arts.

The feast day of St Nicholas (role model for the modern Santa Claus and the bearer of presents on the night of 5 December) is 6 December. In some European countries this is an important time for children (as explained on page 89), but the date is not a significant one in Britain where we must wait until the 25th for our presents.

The shortest day on 21 or 22 December, is no longer part of the Christian Christmas festival but is still commemorated as St Thomas's Day. Previous writers have drawn attention to the similarity between the story of Thomas (in 'the darkness of his unbelief'), who doubted that Jesus would rise again after his crucifixion, and those earlier pagans who doubted that the sun would be born again after the darkness of the winter solstice.

The old ecclesiastical calendar recorded 24 December as the day for decorating churches (*templa exornantur*) and those of a conservative disposition wait until this day before putting up their house decorations. This also marks the beginning of the period formerly known as Christmas-tide.

This day, 24 December, is better known as Christmas Eve. This term still causes some confusion in those who question how the evening could come before the day itself. However, the word 'eve' is not short for 'evening' but refers to the day before an important day. As it happens the 24th is also dedicated to Adam and Eve, which makes the naming of the day doubly significant. The Germanic Christmas tree custom developed from a medieval play about Adam and Eve in which the tree of paradise was represented by a decorated fir tree.

For devout Christians the very start of Christmas Day (from midnight on 24/25 December) is held to be the most sacred. By tradition this was the supposed time of the birth of Jesus, though there is nothing in the scriptures to support this. For most of those who attend midnight mass (the first Christ's Mass of

Christmas, also known as the Angels' Mass and said to have been initiated in the 5th century), the significance of the service time has been lost.

The night between the 24 and 25 of December was obviously an important one even before the birth of Jesus. Among the many earlier pagan customs supplanted by Christianity, not only was 25 December celebrated as the day of the sun's rebirth but the night before, known as Mother's Night, was deemed to be when the Mother actually gave birth to the sun (see page 84).

More people attend church on Christmas Day than on any other day of the year. For Roman Catholics it is still one of the holy days when all must attend a Mass, but until its repeal in the 1960s many millions of people broke a 16th-century law making church attendance on Christmas Day a compulsory act for all. A further act of 1551 made it illegal to play sport on Christmas Day, though this too was later ignored and professional football matches and other sporting meetings continued to be a feature of Christmas Day until the early 1950s.

An early start to Christmas Day is not restricted to those attending midnight mass. It is also a feature of any family with young children, many of whom prove extremely difficult to wake on school days during the dark winter mornings but manage a remarkably early start with their presents on Christmas Day. Christmas dinner (see pages 199 to 221) still means lunch (albeit often at a rather later time than normal) for most, but others prefer to wait until later, when darkness adds an extra bit of magic to the event. While braver souls then reach for the Monopoly set, the bulk of the population spends the rest of the day dozing or watching television – a far cry from earlier times.

THE CUSTOM WAS TRANSFORMED IN VICTORIAN TIMES TO THE CHRISTMAS BOX, A GIFT (OFTEN OF MONEY BUT ALSO OF CLOTHES OR FOOD) GIVEN BY THE UPPER AND MIDDLE CLASSES TO THEIR SERVANTS, LABOURERS AND TRADES-PEOPLE. IT IS THE ORIGIN OF THE CHRISTMAS BONUS.

In 1834 Christmas Day became one of only four days on which the banks closed. The Bank Holiday Act of 1871 extended the official Christmas holiday to include the following day. This day, 26 December, is now generally known as Boxing Day, but prior to the 20th century it was more commonly called St Stephen's Day. Despite being an important day in the sporting calendar it takes its current name not from boxing but from boxes. This can be traced back to the Roman winter festival of Saturnalia, when the money used to pay for the celebrations was saved in pottery boxes.

Later, in medieval times, churches collected money throughout the year to give to the poor and this was kept in special alms-boxes. These were opened on 25 December and distributed on the 26th. Along with many other Christmas customs this one was not left unscathed by the Puritans' brief reign in the mid-17th century. However, many of the landed gentry distributed food to their tenants on 26 December and the box later re-emerged in the form of an earthenware 'piggybank' carried by apprentices in the Christmas season when visiting clients of their master. The clients were expected to give a donation as thanks for the service provided during the year. On Boxing Day the boxes were opened (often by smashing them) and the contents were shared out between the apprentices.

This custom was transformed in Victorian times to the Christmas box, a gift (often of money but also of clothes or food) given by the upper and middle classes to their servants, labourers and trades-people. The tradition lives on in a much-truncated form with the giving of money to those who have delivered the mail or newspapers throughout the year. It is also the origin of the Christmas bonus, given by some firms to their employees, especially those working in the financial sector.

St Stephen's Day is mentioned in the carol *Good King Wenceslas*. It is an important date in the horse racing and hunting calendar and some authors have established a link between this and the fact that St Stephen, who lived in Sweden in the 9th century, is the patron saint of horses. This turns out to be spurious, as the St Stephen whose feast is celebrated on 26 December is not the horse saint but the one that was written about in the Bible (Acts 6: 6–8). This Stephen was the first person to be martyred (c. AD 36) for his fundamental Christian beliefs. Stephen is the patron saint of altar boys, for whom churches used to provide a party on his feast day.

Between Christmas and New Year, on 28 December, is Holy Innocents' Day or Childermas, when the Western Church commemorates the killing of all children under the age of two as ordered by King Herod in his attempt to murder Jesus (see Matthew's account on pages 12 and 13). Eastern branches of the Christian Church commemorate the occasion on 29 December.

New Year's Eve, on 31 December, and the New Year celebrations are usually non-religious in nature, though in Wales and Scotland (page 230) some early Christmas customs seemed to have survived more puritanical times by becoming part of the New Year celebrations. Interestingly, in pagan Anglo-Saxon England, 25 December was regarded as the start of the year. Later, 25 March became the first day of the year. The New Year's Day of 1 January only became universally accepted with the adoption of the Gregorian calendar (page 235).

The evening and night of 5 January, the day *preceding* Epiphany (Twelfth Day) is called Twelfth Night. It is the Twelfth Night *after* Christmas. Epiphany itself is on 6 January and it is the Twelfth Day *after* Christmas. It celebrates the visit of the Magi to the infant Jesus as well as his later baptism and the first miracle at Cana. The Twelfth Day marks the close of the Christian festival and all decorations should be removed by the end of this day. Note that by this reckoning 26 December, the first day *after* Christmas, is the first of the 12 days. Twelfth Night was formerly a very rowdy end to the Christmas celebrations.

Many books state that such festivities actually took place on 6 January, the day of Epiphany. This seems to have arisen because people like a 'day' to begin with morning and so transferred Twelfth Night customs from the evening of 5 January to the day and evening of 6 January.

In the 4th century, the Western Church, which celebrated a 25 December Nativity, and the Eastern Church, which chose 6 January (our Epiphany), adopted a 12-day period of celebration from Christmas to Epiphany. Twelve days also marked the length of the Mesopotamian Marduk celebrations and more northern pagan celebrations. The Yule log burning went on for 12 days, or to be more precise 12 nights. The time at the end of an old year and the beginning of a new one has always been a significant period and one in which evil powers were thought to gain renewed strength. Wassail ceremonies (page 222) took place during the 12 days in attempts to counter the power of evil spirits. The Twelve Days of Christmas represent the last six days of the old year (26 to 31 December) and the first six days of the New Year (1 to 6 January).

In medieval England a special Twelfth Night cake included a bean, the finder of which became the organiser of the night's revelry. Shakespeare's play *Twelfth Night* would have been performed as part of the celebrations at the conclusion of Christmas. It includes a fair degree of drunkenness and buffoonery, typical of Twelfth Night festivities. In 16th- and early-17th-century England the Twelve Days of Christmas were observed in a way more akin to the Roman celebration of Saturnalia. In addition to overeating and drinking it was a time of high spirits. Later, the extended celebrations of the Twelve Days became more subdued.

That the first day of *celebrations* frequently only began *after* the 25 December is alluded to in Thomas Hardy's *Under the Greenwood Tree*:

> 'Dick! Now I cannot – really, I cannot allow any dancing at all till Christmas Day is out,' said old William emphatically.
>
> 'When the clock ha' done striking twelve, dance as much as ye like.'

For most of the Victorian age the consequence of the calendar change in 1752 was that before 1900, Old Christmas Day (Julian calendar) fell on 6 January (by the new Gregorian calendar), which was not only Epiphany but also some 12 days *after* 25 December. So the Twelve Days of Christmas became confused with the 12 days *from* Christmas Day to Old Christmas Day.

Candlemas or Lady Day falls on 2 February and marks the 40th day after the birth of Jesus. This was when Mary went to the Temple to be purified and the day is also known as 'The Purification of Saint Mary the Virgin'. Candles at Candlemas signify the light of Christ to the Gentiles, the day being a recapitulation of the Epiphany, when the infant Jesus was shown to the Magi, representing the Gentiles.

1,500 BRITISH CHRISTMASES

Early Days

I t was during the 3rd and 4th centuries that the Christian Church settled on 25 December as the day to honour Christ's birthday. This was the time of Roman Britain, though, as scholar Norman Davies points out, only 30 per cent of the Isles were under civilian Roman rule – mostly what forms today's England. Before Christianity became a tolerated cult in AD 313, Verulamium of St Alban was martyred for sheltering a fugitive priest.

By the time the Romans withdrew from Britain in the early years of the 5th century there were Christian churches (including one at Canterbury) and chapels in England. In addition, missionaries had spread the word to Wales, Scotland and Ireland, where the Celtic peoples embraced Christianity. Right from the start the mixing of the Christian Christmas with the long-practised customs of the midwinter festivals brought complaints, like those of the 4th century's St Gregory of Nazianzus who expressed concern about overeating and too much dancing at Christmas.

The largely Germanic (Anglo-Saxon) invaders of Britain from the east introduced more pagan customs such as the midwinter Yule ceremony and in AD 597 the Roman Church sent Bishop Augustinius (St Augustine) to reinforce Christianity. Back in Rome, Pope Gregory (Gregorius the Great) instructed his subjects to adapt heathen ideals (including converting animal sacrifices into special meals to the glory of God) rather than trying to counter them openly. One 7th-century king in East Anglia constructed a pagan shrine and a Christian altar in the same building. As such, it is not surprising that many early Christmas customs are a fusion of pagan and Christian practices. In AD 664 at the Synod of Whitby the (largely English) Church accepted the customs (and even the calendar) of the Church in Rome.

The Viking invaders brought old Norse customs and a belief in gods such as Odin (a possible archetype for Father Christmas; see page 80), Thor and Frigg (who, as the wife of Odin, is associated with some of the Christmas mistletoe customs; see page 134). Christianity, however, was far from dormant during this time and, during the 9th-century reign of Alfred the Great, a law was passed setting aside the 12 days after the Nativity for the celebration of the Christmas festival.

William the Conqueror was crowned in Westminster Abbey on Christmas Day, 1066. The Norman kings and their network of barons introduced formality and considerable finance to Christmas celebrations at court. For them, hunting was an important part of the Christmas-tide sport and among the animals pursued was the wild boar, a native creature famed for its strength, speed and ferocity. Its meat became a key ingredient of the Christmas feast. In the 12th century,

THE WILD BOAR HUNT: KILLING THE BOAR

Henry II held sumptuous Christmas feasts at Windsor, one lasting for some nine hours and including delicacies imported from Constantinople (Istanbul), Alexandria and Palestine. Drinks included ale and cider, the latter often mixed with honey or spices. An early carol from this period refers to Christmas drinking and the bidding of wassail (see page 222).

During the time of the Crusades those returning from the Holy Lands brought not just new foodstuffs to our shores but also novel subjects for the seasonal plays that were becoming such an important part of Christmas. The character of Turk in the mummers' presentations is one such addition that stemmed from the Crusades. In the 13th century both King John and later Henry III pushed spending on Christmas to new heights. In 1252 Henry celebrated Christmas together with the marriage of his daughter. More than a thousand knights attended the event and it was perhaps fortunate for the exchequer that the 600 fat oxen slaughtered for the occasion came as a gift from the Archbishop of York.

In 1299 while Edward I was on his way to celebrate Christmas in Scotland he witnessed the ceremony of the Boy Bishop (see pages 89 and 90). Edward III included a Lord of Misrule as part of his very extended Christmas festivities that included much dancing, 'disguisings' and masques – dramatic performances that combined music, mime, verse and scenery. Away from the royal court the barons and other landowners were encouraged to show hospitality to their tenants and others of a lower rank. This not only maintained feudal links but it undoubtedly helped many poorer country people to survive the hardships of winter.

Throughout the 14th and 15th centuries Christmases at court continued to be important events and barometers of new and changing customs. In 1445 Henry VI was entertained by a play reflecting scenes from the Nativity and the playing of cards became a popular **CHRISTMAS MEATS OF THIS TIME INCLUDED SWAN, HERON, CONGER, STURGEON AND PEACOCK.** Christmas pastime. Gambling had been a part of the Roman Saturnalia festival and, though it was banned at all other times of the year during Henry VII's reign, card playing was almost expected as part of the Christmas celebrations. Christmas meats of this time included swan, heron, conger, sturgeon and peacock – the latter served in the presence of nobility as 'peacock enkakyll' with the roasted flesh coloured with cinnamon before being sewn back into its skin and feathers.

The court of Henry VIII was treated to great tournaments, masques and Nativity plays as part of a prolonged period of celebrating Christmas. This too was the time when the London Inns of Court appointed a Lord of Misrule to oversee their Christmas antics, while several of the Oxford colleges did the same. In 1534 Henry rejected the power of the Pope in Rome and also suppressed the election of Boy Bishops. The custom was revived under the Catholic Queen Mary who was sung to by the Boy Bishop of St Paul's on both

St Nicholas's Day (6 December) and Holy Innocents' Day (28 December).

For the second half of the 16th century Elizabeth I continued the boisterous celebrations in the vein of her father Henry. At times fear of contracting plague prevented her from holding court at 'Grenwych' but the festivities were simply transferred to Hampton Court. Among her favourite activities at this time was playing at dice. It is said that she invariably beat her contestants because her dice were loaded in favour of the high numbers. The delights of the royal Christmas at court kept too many country landowners away from their estates, to the detriment of their tenants at Christmas, and Elizabeth later commanded her courtiers to 'repair to their counties, and there to keep hospitality amongst their neighbours'.

We get some idea about Christmas food from the Elizabethan poet Thomas Tusser:

Christmas Husbandry Fare

Beef, mutton, and pork, shred pies of the best,
Pig, veal, goose, and capon, and turkey well
dressed
Cheese, apples, and nuts, jolly carols to hear,
As then in the country is counted good cheer.

(Shred pies = mince pies; see page 218. Note that the turkey had arrived – see page 205.)

The extravagant Royal Christmas celebrations of the 15th and 16th centuries were largely non-religious in nature, as were the more simple festivities kept by those lower down the social hierarchy. Little had changed by the early part of the 17th century when Robert Herrick (vicar of Dean Prior in Devon) recounted:

> ... a jolly
> Verse crowned with ivy and holly;
> That tells of winter's tales and mirth,
> That milk-maids make about the hearth,
> Of Christmas sports, the Wassail bowl,
> That's tossed up after Fox-i'-th'-hole:
> Of Blind-man's-buff, and of the care
> That young men have to shoe the mare:
> Of Twelfth-tide cake, of peas and beans,
> Wherewith you make those merry scenes,
> And thus, throughout, with Christmas plays,
> Frolic the full twelve holy-days.

By the time James I came to the throne in 1603 the Puritan movement in the now Reformed Church of England was becoming more powerful. Puritans pointed to the excesses of Christmas in their drive to rid the Protestant Church of pagan-based rituals and feast days celebrated in the manner of the Roman Catholic Church. Despite this, James enjoyed a number of Christmas masques written by Ben Jonson. James's attempt to remodel the Scottish Church, including the compulsory observation of Christmas as a feast day, was not well received and during the ensuing reign of Charles I the Scottish Presbyterians joined forces with the English 'Roundheads' in defeating the Royalist 'Cavaliers' during the Civil War.

The increased power of parliament (with its many Puritan sympathisers) following the defeat of the Royalists resulted in a number of laws restricting the excesses of what became known as 'Old Christmas'. The first of these 'ordinances' was actually issued in the year the Civil War started (1642) and concerned the suppression of plays at Christmas. By Christmas 1643 some shops in London stayed open on Christmas Day and in 1644 Christmas Day was declared by parliament to be a day of fasting, not feasting. The year 1645 was the first under the new Anglican prayer book in which Christmas was not designated as a day for holding church services. On Christmas Day every good citizen was expected to open his shop as usual and compel his apprentices to keep behind the counter.

To make their point, parliament even sat on Thursday, 25 December – *The Weekly Account* baldly stating, 'The Commons sate in a Grande Committee concerning privileges of the members of their House.' In spite of this, the celebration of Christmas went on behind closed doors, especially in country areas. For many, such as apprentices and labourers, the loss of free food and other goods was more serious than the suppression of the fun and games associated with Old Christmas.

By 1647 Christmas was banned altogether, with no evergreens and no church. These further restrictions led to riots, especially in Canterbury where a resolution was passed that if the people could not have their Christmas Day they were determined to have the King on his throne again. Far from regaining the throne, Charles was executed in 1649. During the following decade the celebration of Christmas went underground.

John Evelyn recorded in his diary for 25 December 1657 that whilst attending a private service the chapel was surrounded by soldiers who detained everyone. He was only released after being questioned as to why he had offended against the ordinance that none should any longer observe the superstitious time of the Nativity.

The Restoration of the monarchy, when Charles II was crowned in 1660, meant that Christmas celebrations were allowed again, though the Scots continued to make much more of the New Year. With Charles II as King, *Poor Robin's Almanack* printed the following:

Now thanks to God for Charles' return,
Whose absence made old Christmas mourn:
For then we scarcely did it know,
Whether it Christmas were or no.

Charles was a great lover of the traditional English Christmas dish, the baron of beef, consisting of two sirloins. Sirloin comes from two old French words meaning over loin but many prefer the anecdotal story of Charles knighting his beloved beef loin, hence 'arise sir-loin'. Though attempts were made to revive the former splendour of Christmas entertainment at court it was noticeable that these and those held by the nobility rarely reached the same heights as those prior to the Puritans' rule. As the new century dawned under William and Mary, *Poor Robin's Almanack* commented:

Christmas 1701

But the times are grown so bad
Scarce one dish for the poor is had:
Good housekeeping is laid aside,
And all is spent to maintain pride:
Good works are counted popish, and
Small charity is in the land.
A man may sooner (truth I tell you)
Break his own neck than fill his belly.
Good God amend what is amiss
And send a remedy to this,
That Christmas day again may rise
And we enjoy our Christmas pies.

Christmas under George I saw a novel innovation, that of the play that was to give rise to the modern pantomime. The major change under George II came about in 1752 when the new Gregorian calendar was introduced to Britain. Many people refused to observe the festival 11 days earlier in the season (though still on 25 December) and instead held their celebrations on Old Christmas Day that, prior to 1800, fell on 5 January. In the second half of the 18th century the Revd Dr William Stukeley's fascination with the Druids led to a renewed interest in mistletoe and its place in Christmas decorations (see page 135).

Gradually Christmas-tide became a quieter occasion, though Twelfth Night remained the most boisterous part of the festival. For some people Christmas Day became an ordinary working day. A leader in *The Times* of 1790 commented, 'within the last half century this annual time of festivity has lost much of its original mirth and hospitality'. Part of this decline was due to social upheavals of the time. These included greater mobility and an accelerating drift from the country towards urban areas. Local customs were left behind in a time when outsiders purchased many of our country estates. Such people lacked the family traditions of providing Christmas hospitality in the countryside.

The Victorian Christmas – Class, Charity and the First Scrooges

Only a few years before Victoria came to the throne in 1837 did Christmas become more of a celebration. The Victorian Christmas evolved over the last six decades of the 19th century as a combination of old traditions (often watered down), newly imported customs and novel innovations. What had been largely a series of outdoor communal events, with many local village customs, became an indoor family event. Above all, Christmas was to become much more of a children's festival.

Class played a part in this. The landed gentry who offered hospitality from their large houses had been an important part of pre-19th century Christmases, but it was the new urban middle class, including doctors, bankers, merchants and shopkeepers, who were at the forefront of the Victorian Christmas revival. It was at this group of people that one of the great spin-doctors of his age was to aim his writing. The accounts of Christmas celebrations in the short stories and novels of Charles Dickens still epitomise the spirit of a Victorian Christmas.

In *Pickwick Papers* (1836), Dickens looked back nostalgically to an idealised Old Christmas (more typical of the 16th and 17th centuries), with country gentlemen arranging huge parties to the accompaniment of musicians and roaring log fires. Later *A Christmas Carol* (1843) dealt more with a contemporary urban Christmas and the social injustices between the newly created middle and working classes as found in the mushrooming cities of early Victorian Britain. The book pricked the social conscience of the middle classes and this helped it to sell some 15,000 copies in its first year of publication. The appearance of spirits in the story appealed to those who associated the dark days of Christmas-tide with ghost stories.

Christmas charity had previously taken the form of the stately home party and food distribution for the country poor. This spirit was now being mirrored in the city. Middle-class citizens gave donations to movements such as the Salvation Army to help the urban poor. Queen Victoria set the example. She arranged for beef portions, decorated with sprigs of holly from Windsor Castle, to be distributed to the elderly and poor. Similar handouts took place at Sandringham, while at the Queen's Osborne estate on the Isle of Wight, her labourers' children received gifts of gloves and cloaks.

In London and many other cities, thousands of poor people were given free meals on Christmas Day. Others were treated to money (often half a sovereign), joints of beef, plum puddings or clothing. These distributions often took place on St Thomas's Day (just before Christmas). Special meals were laid on for those in prison over Christmas. Toys were collected and given out to those children unfortunate enough to be spending Christmas in hospital.

As always, there were those who were less enamoured of Christmas, as typified by Benjamin Haydon who, in his diary for 25 December 1846, wrote of Christmas:

> I hate the vulgar revelry which usually accompanies it – the fat beef, the gross turkeys, the stuffed sausage, as evidence of human joy at the Salvation of Christ – are to me utterly

disgusting! – But my boys will consider me a brute if I don't eat till I can't see, to prove my joy at their presence.

Travel became more reliable and cheaper as stagecoaches were replaced by the railways which spread rapidly after 1840. This encouraged the family gatherings that were to become such a key feature of the Victorian Christmas. The railways also helped to create national rather than local Christmas customs and the Union flag became a part of Christmas decorations. As part of the nostalgia for 'Old Christmas', stagecoaches featured in many of the stories by Dickens.

As the importance of commerce grew and Britain became 'a nation of shopkeepers' so Christmas presents especially for children, became more central to the celebrations. From the 1860s, present giving, which had been associated with New Year, began to be transferred to Christmas. Some of the more boisterous customs such as the Lord of Misrule were quietly dropped as family customs became more important. As we shall see on page 97 the importation of the American Santa Claus (by the 1870s) helped to reinvigorate our earlier Father Christmas figure in the now more child-orientated Christmas. The Christmas pantomime developed in Victorian times from its antecedents, becoming much closer to its current format. In doing so it became a firm favourite with middle-class families in London and other cities.

Much of the imagery and many of the customs associated with the modern Christmas celebrations in Britain can be traced back to the Victorian era. Taking their cue from Victoria and Albert, the people embraced the Christmas tree, a custom imported from Germany but they also revived and repackaged older national Christmas customs, especially carols and initiated new ones that have since spread round the world.

One of many Victorian innovations was the commercial Christmas card although as with Christmas toys many of these were later imported from Germany. The Christmas cracker was another Victorian invention. The idealised White Christmas weather also comes to us from the Victorians and especially the writings of Dickens. Elements of the Christmas fare, decorations and entertainment were all transformed during this time, thus laying the foundation for our modern celebration.

Wartime and More Recent Christmases

A little over a hundred years since the death of Queen Victoria, Christmas has continued to move with the times. Some customs, such as mumming and guising, that survived through the 19th century are now confined to a few places where they have become tourist attractions. Conversely, new inventions such as television have transformed the pattern of activities on

Christmas Day for much of the population, with James Bond supplanting the Queen in the affections of many UK households.

The first half of the 20th century was dominated by two World Wars. There are numerous accounts, from many different wars all over the world, of the difficulties encountered by those trying to celebrate Christmas on the battlefront. In addition, the shortage of goods, disturbance to routines and mental anguish felt by loved ones back home all resulted in a very different Christmas during wartime. There is something ironic about accounts of war during a time associated with feelings of peace and 'goodwill to all men'. Sadly, religious differences under the guise of nationalism have been the root cause of many wars.

During December 1914, Pope Benedict attempted to broker an armistice during what was to be the first of the Great War's four Christmases. The official armistice never came about, partly because, at the time, no side was winning or saw any advantage in a cessation of fighting. A less obvious reason for the failure of the Christmas truce was that not all the forces fighting the war celebrated Christmas on the same day. Followers of the Orthodox Church still adhered to the old Julian calendar, under which their Christmas Day was some 13 days after that celebrated by both the British and German forces, who adhered to the Gregorian calendar's 25 December (see pages 234 to 236). Bulgaria and Turkey (fighting on the German side) did not change to the Gregorian calendar until 1916 and

1919, respectively. Russia (fighting against the Germans) also did not change until 1919.

As it happened, an *unofficial* Christmas truce between German and Allied troops (British, French and Belgian forces) did occur in 1914 along sections of the Western Front in Flanders. The truce was not spontaneous but followed weeks of incidents when the closeness of the opposing forces (sometimes as little as 60m apart) facilitated shouted communication between the troops and even the exchange of newspapers (thrown across, tied round a stone).

Such fraternisation (the official term) was not encouraged by the more senior ranks and one commanding officer issued instructions forbidding such events, claiming that they would discourage initiative in commanders and destroy the offensive spirit in all ranks. Among the prohibited actions were any 'friendly intercourse with the enemy, unofficial armistices and the exchange of tobacco and other comforts'. It now seems likely that, in most cases, the temporary truce negotiations were initiated by the German ranks. Many Germans had worked in Britain before the war and during its early stages there was less deep-rooted animosity between the two sides. The German troops were certainly well supplied with Christmas fare. One local truce started when German soldiers placed Christmas trees on the parapets of their trenches. In places, shouted invitations of 'come over here' and sign boards spelling out 'you no fight, we no fight' resulted in the coming together of the troops in no man's land.

The meetings frequently resulted in exchanges of gifts including cigarettes, food and alcohol, along with newspapers and the swapping of tunic buttons. Singing, either together or from nearby trenches, was also common and on one occasion the Germans' rendition of *Stille Nacht* (*Silent Night*) brought applause from the Allied troops.

Truce

It begins with one or two soldiers,
And one or two following
With hampers over their shoulders.
They might be off wild fowling

As they would another Christmas Day,
So gingerly they pick their steps.
No one seems sure of what to do.
All stop when one stops.

A fire gets lit. Some spread
Their greatcoats on the frozen ground.
Polish vodka, fruit and bread
Are broken out and passed round.

The air of an old German song,
The rules of Patience, are the secrets
They'll share before long.
They draw on their last cigarettes

As Friday night lovers, when it's over,
Might get up from their mattresses
To congratulate each other
And exchange names and addresses.

(Paul Muldoon)

In some places the coming together of men from the opposing trenches allowed both sides to identify and bury their dead, a task that was extremely dangerous and often impossible under normal battle conditions. In one case, while the Chaplain of the Gordon Highlanders was negotiating such an arrangement a hare (some reports say a rabbit) was seen between the two lines and was chased by men from both sides before being captured (and no doubt eaten) by the Germans. The Chaplain, one Revd Adams, later conducted a short burial service which included the 23rd Psalm.

In January 1915 an officer in the London Rifle Brigade wrote to *The Times* about one Christmas truce: 'on Christmas Day a football match was played between them and us in front of the trench', and there are other stories of matches played with makeshift balls. The official history of the London Rifle Brigade makes no mention of a match but this may be because a brief kick-about is not everyone's idea of a match.

Most of the truces were short-lived and few lasted for more than 48 hours. The reaction of high-ranking soldiers and politicians on both sides was that the recurrence of such truces was to be strongly discouraged. From 1915 to the end of the war, both sides went to great lengths to provide seasonal food and entertainment at Christmas, partly to prevent any more Christmas truces. By this time, too, most of the troops had experienced the loss of close friends and attitudes between the sides had hardened.

That the soldiers of the opposing forces could make friends, however briefly, was an embarrassment to politicians and senior commanders. 'FOES IN TRENCHES SWAP PIES FOR WINE' was a typical paper headline but many reports made very little comment on the truces. Official accounts often made little or no mention of the events and even denied that they had ever happened. By the Second World War people were left wondering whether the 1914 stories were fictitious – showing the effectiveness of the propaganda machine.

Later wars have also seen truces, but even where these have been more official than those in 1914, senior politicians were loath to admit to having anything to do with them. So when, in 1972, following a 36-hour Christmas suspension of the American bombing over North Vietnam, President Nixon returned to the White House on Boxing Day he made no public acknowledgement that there had been a suspension of the bombing.

For those on the front line, reminders of a normal Christmas were good for morale, hence the attempts at providing 'turkey' (often rabbit) and especially Christmas pudding. Where possible, extra deliveries of mail from home were arranged to coincide with the Christmas celebrations. Entertainment was laid on and pantomime was popular, especially that produced by the combatants themselves when much of the humour related to the inevitable cross-dressing. In the Second World War, professional entertainers performed for the troops and there were frequent film shows.

Rationing and the shortage of goods often resulted in even less traditional fare for those back home than for the troops. By the latter part of the Second World War, a Christmas bird was a rare treat in urban Britain and a lack of imported dried fruit, together with a shortage of butter and fresh eggs, resulted in many interesting recipes for the puddings and pies of Christmas. Rabbit followed by carrot cake was the closest many people came to a Christmas lunch. Toys were also in short supply, resulting in high prices. The 'make do and mend' mentality was much in evidence.

Between the wars a more normal Christmas returned. Replying to a friend on 27 December 1918, D. H. Lawrence wrote that he had received the parcel from this friend on Christmas morning: in fact, he had encountered the postman on setting off for a walk.

More than 80 years on from Lawrence's account the Christmas Day postal delivery is but a distant memory for older people: the last Christmas Day delivery was in 1961. Fewer still can remember when national daily papers were published on Christmas Day, a practice that ceased in 1912. Post workers, newspaper deliverers and others such as public transport workers are all now able to take part in the holiday.

By the end of the 20th century the almost total shutdown of public transport on Christmas Day, together with only limited services on the surrounding days, had resulted in a huge increase in the number of car journeys made as a consequence of family visits at Christmas. In 2001 the AA estimated that some 20 million cars would be on the road in Britain over the Christmas period. Up to the middle of the 20th century many Christmas celebrations involved the coming together of extended families including grandparents, uncles, aunts and their children. By the beginning of the 21st century the typical get-together only consisted of more immediate family members. Party numbers have been further diminished by an overall reduction in family size. The average number of children per couple has halved from 3.4 in 1900 to just 1.7 a hundred years later.

Other trends have necessitated more travel at Christmas. Young adults are now much less likely to find work and settle in the same community as their parents, so a family Christmas involves more than just local travel. The huge increase in divorce rates, single-parent families and the number of children from second (and subsequent) partnerships has resulted in the complex shuttling of children between parents, step-parents and ex-parents so that all can share time together (but not be all together) at Christmas. The jokes about the choice of parents or parents-in-law for the family Christmas visit have become outdated in a time of increasingly complex relationships.

The decline of public services on Christmas Day has been mirrored by the loss of public entertainment such as sporting fixtures, concerts, pantomime and film performances. League football matches were a feature of Christmas Day before the Second World War, but the post-war revival of such fixtures ceased in the late 1950s, following complaints from the families of players. Between the wars cinemas in some cities (including my adopted home of Sheffield) screened Christmas morning specials, some of which were reserved for the city's poorest children.

With the notable exception of the import from America (in the final two decades of the 20th century) of the custom of using Christmas lights and other decorations to fill gardens, roofs and the outer walls of houses, Christmas Day has become more and more an inside event. The changes outlined above have furthered the cause of the 'stay at home Christmas' and resulted in a quieter celebration, far removed from the boisterous occasions of former times. Even the pre-Christmas bands of carol-singing school children have declined in number as modern parents worry about their children's exposure to road accidents, or attacks on dark winter evenings. Far from resulting in an increase in time spent playing indoor family games even the Monopoly set has not been able to resist the advance of television.

The Victorian ideal of Christmas as being a time to

make charitable donations and offer practical help to those less well-off is still with us. Organisations such as Crisis (at Christmas) provide shelter, food and clothing to the London homeless over the Christmas period. Such operations reflect those that were a feature of Christmas over a hundred years ago. The sale of charity Christmas cards provides a salve to the conscience of those concerned that the high spending and enforced happiness surrounding the modern Christmas only broaden the gap between those who have (money, good health and so on) and those who have not.

IN THE 1930s SANTA WAS DEPICTED WITH A CIGARETTE BETWEEN HIS LIPS AS PART OF AN ADVERTISING CAMPAIGN.

Father Christmas and Santa Claus were transformed, hybridised and commercialised during the 20th century. In the 1930s Santa was even depicted with a cigarette between his lips as part of an advertising campaign for the 'Craven A' brand. This was an interesting throwback to his pipe-smoking American origins. Other changes have been subtler, especially with regard to decorations, food and drink. The Christmas trees on offer are no longer limited to rootless Norway spruces as other conifers become more fashionable. Artificial trees are available in green, blue, silver and even black. These can have built-in illumination in the form of fibre optics, while, for natural trees, the traditional candles have been replaced by lights of many colours, some flashing in time to Christmas music.

Coloured chains made at home from gummed paper strips have been replaced by ready-made imports. Even the fragile glass baubles, so carefully packed in tissue paper for 11 months of the year, are being usurped by slightly less fragile wooden and straw objects, more typical of the traditions of other European countries. The Christmas tree star has found a new guise as a hanging light shade and the seven-stepped candle-lights have spread from being a uniquely Jewish custom to become a Christmas windowsill feature. The wassail bowl has been replaced by New World wine and even the early 20th-century fad for egg-nog at Christmas has sunk under the weight of lager, Red Bull and other more trendy drinks.

Cheap, oven-ready turkeys and shop-bought Christmas puddings have greatly assisted in the move to reduce preparation time for Christmas food, a trend that has accelerated in the past few decades along with the huge increase in the percentage of working women. Recently, the more affluent have turned to organically reared fresh birds and turkey alternatives, including goose and even wild boar. Beef, another traditional English dish at Christmas, suffered a temporary setback during the BSE (mad cow) crisis.

In the 1940s only about 100,000 people applied for a special vegetarian ration book, but by the first full survey in 1984 there were over a million vegetarians, a figure that has since risen to over 3 million. Nut loaves and Quorn-based turkey lookalikes are now a more prominent part of many Christmas menus. Delia Smith has restored the cranberry (though now as a cultivated American import in place of our wild crop – see page 212) to its former glory. Christmas pudding is less popular and the trend for the sweet course is towards more stollen, chocolate roulade and also to serving foods with a lower calorie count.

Favourites from the 1950s and 1960s, including crystallised ginger, Newberry Fruits and liqueur chocolates, have all but vanished to be replaced by Belgian biscuits and chocolate truffles. Even the simple clementine now has competition from satsumas and other 'easy to eat' oranges. The rise of the supermarket and the use of promotional offers have been instrumental in many of the innovations outlined above. The potted Christmas has seen similar changes. No middle-class house in the 1950s and 1960s was complete without the Christmas berry plant but these wilted under the onslaught of red poinsettias. Today a range of different-coloured poinsettia cultivars (varieties) is being challenged by Christmas newcomers such as the moth orchid.

The spread of new technology is having a strong influence on Christmas at the start of the new millennium. Examples of this include the growing popularity of the Christmas e-mail as a replacement for cards, the dominance of computer games over more traditional toys and the increased choice of Christmas viewing as more people sign up for multi-channel television. New technology has helped to bring about a much greater uniformity across all parts of Britain in the way Christmas is spent. Recently, the first Christmas shops have opened in this country, another import from the North American continent where the year-round Christmas store is a feature of many big cities.

What is certain is that Christmas will not stay the same. For all those who bemoan the loss of a 'traditional Christmas' one can point to similar statements made down the centuries. Christmas has survived, unlike many of the other seasonal celebrations, partly because it has changed with the times, and no doubt it will continue to evolve over the coming centuries.

SANTA CLAUS IS COMING TO TOWN

Father Christmas and his Long-lost Companion

Father Christmas has often been seen as a British St Nicholas, but a glimpse at the role of Father Christmas in medieval England shows this to be inaccurate. In fact, the stories from which the personality of Father Christmas has emerged pre-date not only Nicholas but even the Nativity. As with many Christian Christmas customs, the tale of the present-giving St Nicholas satisfied the desire of early missionaries to replace pagan traditions with comparable church-based ones. The saintly bearer of winter gifts actually had many, much older, pagan models.

In his fascinating book *When Santa Was a Shaman*, Tony van Renterghem suggests that, long before any form of organised religion, providing spiritual guidance for small groups of our ancestors was a principal task of the shaman – better known as the medicine man or woman. Such people were the embodiment of our modern priest, doctor, astronomer and artisan combined. Their role was to communicate with the gods and so bring gifts of knowledge (especially in the hunt for food) and healing to their people.

The ritual pre-hunt dances performed by shamans wearing horns or antlers are represented in 12,000-year-old French cave paintings. These figures were later embodied in medieval Britain by characters like Pan and Herne who, like their predecessors, encouraged sexual freedom. This was portrayed by the besom (broom) they carried. The broom became a symbol representing the sex-organs and to 'jump the broomstick' signified a marriage not sanctioned by the church. Early images of Father Christmas often show him carrying a broom and depict him as a shaman-like Pan figure.

We can trace the roots of Allfather, the original pagan god of the sky, back at least 6,000 years to a time when he may have evolved from some of the great shamans. Allfather appears again as the chief Norse god Odin, also known as Wotan or Woden. He was a father figure to his people, associated with the arrival of winter but also as the bearer of gifts. In Scandinavian mythology he is shown as the Old Man of Winter who sweeps into the lowlands bringing snow and driving the reindeer herds on their migration. As leader of the hunt Odin was typically depicted with a long white beard, wearing a cloak and hat, holding a spear and riding through the skies on his pale grey, eight-legged horse known as Sleipner. More significantly, he travelled with a Dark Helper, a horned, Pan-like figure. The Helper severely castigated those who had been bad, in marked contrast to the helpful gifts given by Odin to those who had been good.

In southern Europe, Odin's role was taken by the Greek god Zeus and the Roman gods Mercury and Saturn. We've already seen how the Roman midwinter festival of Saturnalia and the closely linked New Year festival included many of the less religious elements of the Christmas celebrations. These include the giving of presents and the election of a mock king, the Lord of Misrule, to help organise the festivities.

While many European countries inadvertently incorporated some earlier pagan features in their St Nicholas figures, Britain stuck with a Father Christmas (he was also known as Yule) who, though incorporating the St Nicholas story, was closer to the pagan Lord of Misrule figure and was associated with the Twelve Days of Christmas rather than the 6 December feast day of Nicholas.

St Nicholas was revered in Britain but Father Christmas remained the important Christmas character. One 15th-century carol began 'Hail Father Christmas, hail to thee'. Father Christmas also appeared as a character in the mummers' plays:

In comes I, Father Christmas
Welcome or welcome not.
I hope old Father Christmas
Will never be forgot.

Following the Crusades the plays often included a fight between St George and a character called the Turk. In many plays Father Christmas was the narrator, a sort of Lord of Misrule who also appeared near the end of the performance under the guise of the Doctor, who brought back to life the character slain in the fight scene. This has elements both of earlier shamanic beliefs and the resurrection story of the boys in the barrel, associated with St Nicholas.

Following the Reformation, Father Christmas (and Saint Nicholas) became less important in most Protestant countries in Europe. In Ben Jonson's *Christmas His Masque*, as performed at the 17th-century court of James I, the character of Christmas was described as having a long thin beard and bearing a truncheon (a replacement for the earlier broom?). The performance took place a mere 20 years before attempts by the Puritans to ban the celebration of Christmas, which they saw as a combination of Catholic and pagan customs. Certainly by this time Father Christmas (also known as Captain Christmas) was just that strange mix.

In Jonson's masque the character of Christmas asks why people should keep him out and pleads, 'Why I am no dangerous person ... though I come out of Pope's

Head Alley, as good a Protestant as any i' my parish.' Christmas is obviously fearful of his Catholic (St Nicholas) ancestry but feels he also has a place in the Protestant church. His more pagan past is alluded to in the play in which one of his children is called Misrule.

The Father Christmas figure was suppressed by Cromwell but he reappeared following the restoration of the monarchy. Not surprisingly, Father Christmas had lost most traces of his Catholic ancestry by then and reverted to a more Saturnalian (or even Bacchanalian) character. Vestiges of this may be seen in the figure of the Ghost of Christmas Present in Dickens' *A Christmas Carol*, published in 1843.

Another snapshot of the Old Father Christmas in the mid-19th century (shortly before the American Santa Claus figure arrived) is provided in a poem written in 1850 by Mary Howitt:

Welcome to Christmas

He comes – the brave old Christmas!
His sturdy steps I hear;
We give him a hearty welcome,
For he comes but once a year!

Oh, he is a fine old fellow
His heart's in the truest place;
You may know that at once by the children,
Who glory to see his face.

For he never forgets the children,
They all are dear to him;
You'll see that with wonderful presents
His pockets are crammed to the brim.

Fifty years ago an effigy of Father Christmas was hung from the railings of Dijon Cathedral before being burnt in the presence of several hundred Sunday-school children. Father Christmas's crime was that of paganising the Christmas festival and eclipsing the Nativity as the most important part of Christmas. At least the French were prepared to acknowledge his pagan past.

While Father Christmas in one form or another lived on as a direct descendant of the original sky god Allfather, what had been happening to the original Earth goddess? Mother Earth, as she was known, lived on for many thousands of years in different guises, including Nerthus, Frigg (see this Norse goddess's connection with the mistletoe

FIFTY YEARS AGO AN EFFIGY OF FATHER CHRISTMAS WAS HUNG FROM THE RAILINGS OF DIJON CATHEDRAL BEFORE BEING BURNT.

story on page 134) and Freya (the goddess of love and beauty in Scandinavian mythology). Nerthus and Freya were believed to tour the countryside just after midwinter and as such both epitomised a Mother Christmas figure. Bede, the great 7th-century chronicler of Saxon England, wrote that the night before Christmas was known as Mother's Night. In the church calendar 24 December is the Day of Adam and Eve, commemorating the first father and mother in the creation story.

One of the great Viking sagas gives us an account of Mother's Night in the 10th century with a woman (Mother Christmas?) dressed in a long cloak, complete with a black hood, lined with white cat-skin. She carried a staff, symbolic of the World Tree (Yggdrasil) that was believed to connect the heavens above with the Earth and spirit world beneath. Like the shamans and her male god counterparts she was able to travel to the spirit worlds and so seek advice for those on Earth. She would then foretell future harvest prospects and details of personal fortunes.

By the Middle Ages, Mother Christmas had largely disappeared, overwhelmed by the march of Father Christmas. Feminists should perhaps have warmed to 20th-century Russia where Father Christmas was replaced by the communists with a New Year present-giver called Grandfather Frost alongside a reincarnated Mother Christmas in the guise of his grand-daughter, the Ice Maiden. More interestingly an older Russian story involves another Mother Christmas figure, the witch-like present-giver known as Baba Yaga.

Saint Nicholas, Man and Myth

One Christmas legend is probably more widely known than any other, that of St Nicholas as the role model for Santa Claus, the modern bearer of Christmas gifts for children. The story of Nicholas is told in many books in as many different ways, typical of a myth that has been over 1,600 years in the making. All sources seem to agree that Nicholas died on 6 December, though the exact year of his death (early or mid-4th century) is less clear. He is understood to have come from the Turkish (Ancient Lycian) seaport of Patara. Accounts speak of the baby Nicholas standing up in his bath on the first day of his life and only feeding from his mother's breast on Wednesdays and Fridays.

When his parents died they left the young man well off. Nicholas was a devout Christian and attended his local church every day. Following the death of the Bishop of Myra (the coastal region of Demre today) a committee was guided to appoint as the next bishop the first person to enter this church on the following day. The first person to arrive was Nicholas and he became the new bishop. Many of the legends that surround Bishop Nicholas centre around his miraculous deeds and charitable acts, the latter with the common element that Nicholas gave away his riches in secret.

Among the former are stories that involved Nicholas saving the lives of sailors whose ships had been caught in violent storms. Another tells of two (or three) boys travelling to Myra to be blessed by Nicholas, who were robbed and murdered by the innkeeper where they slept (other versions say the murderer was a butcher). The dismembered bodies were then supposedly hidden in a barrel of brine. Nicholas is said to have called on God to raise them up and the children were restored to life.

The story that was to associate Nicholas with Christmas concerned an impoverished nobleman in the Myra district who could not afford the dowries needed for the marriages of his three daughters. The man was so poor that he even considered prostituting the girls as a way of bringing money into the household. Nicholas, on hearing of the family's problem, is said to have provided a bag of gold to pay for the eldest daughter's wedding but, as was his practice, he did this secretly; in this case by tossing the bag through an open window at night.

The procedure was successfully repeated for the middle daughter, but a problem arose as the youngest daughter required her dowry in the winter when the window was firmly shut at night. Nicholas solved this problem by quietly climbing on to the roof of the house and dropping the bag of gold down the chimney. Some say it landed in a stocking that was hung up to dry by the fire, others that it landed in a shoe.

Nicholas was buried in Myra and within 200 years of his death the cult of Nicholas had spread far. On being made a Catholic saint his feast day was celebrated on 6 December. Portraits of St Nicholas dating from 6th-century Byzantine churches show him with a long, white beard. He was one of the most loved of the minor saints and quickly became patron saint of children, prostitutes and sailors, among others. It is possible that the seafaring Vikings helped to transport the Nicholas cult to more northern parts of Europe. Accounts also record that prior to invading England, the fleet of William the Conqueror was hit by a bad storm and William called for protection from St

Nicholas. If so, it is perhaps apt that William's coronation in 1066 took place on Christmas Day.

A few years later Myra and the area around it fell to the Muslims. In 1087 the remains of Nicholas were removed from Myra and taken for safe keeping to Bari in Italy, where his supposed relics still lie. This act further enhanced his popularity and by the Middle Ages his cult had extended to many parts of Europe.

Customs surrounding his reputation for charitable giving included hanging up a stocking or putting out a shoe in the anticipation that it would be filled with gifts on the night before the feast of St Nicholas, that is, the night between 5 and 6 December. The tall, slim, bearded St Nicholas, clad in his mitre and grey bishop's cloak, was depicted clasping his staff (crosier) and travelling through the skies on a horse (the latter, with feet firmly on the ground, would have been the common mode of transport in 4th-century Asia Minor). Nicholas would then come down a chimney and secretly leave gifts for all those children who knew their prayers. Apart from the strange habit of travelling on a flying horse, the other components of the story come from the tale (recounted on page 86) of the nobleman and his three daughters.

The benevolent figure of St Nicholas has been the subject of many paintings and other works of art. In these he is often shown assisted by a chained servant, an almost slave-like figure called the Dark Helper. As explained on page 80, this figure had long been associated with the pagan god Odin, the old Norse present-bringer. In southern Germany the Dark Helper is still known as Pelz Nickel (fur-clad Nick) or Knecht Ruprechte (servant Ruprechte) where the rather frightening figure is usually shown brandishing a besom. A broom was also carried by the much more ancient shaman-based Father Christmas figure. Younger children are often frightened by the helper figure and recently adults playing the Ruprechte role have been asked to discard their brooms. In some countries the church tried to banish the Dark Helper figure or portray him as chained to, and thus subservient to, Nicholas.

In many parts of Europe the St Nicholas ceremonies still take place, almost three weeks before Christmas, and are part of local culture. This is especially true in Belgium, southern Germany and even more so in the Netherlands where St Nicholas, known locally as Sinter Claes, arrives by boat, accompanied by one or more 'Black Peters' who carry birch rods. The boat, said to come from Spain, docks just prior to the eve of his feast day. Shoes (preferably the traditional clog) are left out containing carrots and hay for Nicholas's horse. Some also leave a glass of gin for Nicholas, but by tradition this sober man would not have drunk alcohol. The offerings are then 'miraculously' and secretly replaced by presents (for all good children) by the following morning.

IN THE NETHERLANDS SHOES ARE LEFT OUT CONTAINING CARROTS AND HAY FOR NICHOLAS'S HORSE. THE OFFERINGS ARE THEN 'MIRACULOUSLY' AND SECRETLY REPLACED BY PRESENTS.

Historically, St Nicholas was also revered in Britain where over 400 churches (many in coastal parishes) are dedicated to him. In medieval times many churches and cathedrals would elect a Boy Bishop from the rank of younger choristers. An ordination service held on 6 December gave the 'mock' bishop his powers and one such service was witnessed by Edward I in 1299. Boy Bishops were dressed in the attire of a bishop and were allowed to preach (but not officiate at mass) throughout their reign. This reign encompassed Christmas and only came to an end on 28 December – Holy Innocents' Day. The election of a Boy Bishop mimics a much older element of the Roman Saturnalia festival, but the church version resulted in a more sober and less licentious period than that governed by the earlier Lord of Misrule. The Boy Bishop custom was outlawed by Henry VIII. Following its revival it was further suppressed under Cromwell and the Puritans in the mid-17th century.

Enter Santa Claus and the Proof that he Exists

In the 1860s St Nicholas returned from America under a new guise. To catch up with this part of the story we have to go back to the 17th century and some of North America's early European settlers. In 1620 a group of English Puritans sailed for America, where they founded a colony in New England. These

Pilgrim Fathers rejected what they saw as pagan and Catholic influences on Christmas. In keeping Christmas as a more sacred day they transferred the feasting to a form of harvest thanksgiving towards the end of November. In 1863, Abraham Lincoln declared the last Thursday in November a national holiday and, since 1941, Thanksgiving, complete with turkey and pumpkin pie, has been celebrated on the fourth Thursday in November.

Settlers from other European countries arrived with different customs and ideals. By the 17th century, the Netherlands, unlike most other Protestant countries, had maintained its association with Nicholas, a Catholic saint. So when Dutch emigrants founded the American east-coast port of New Amsterdam, they brought their St Nicholas customs with them. In 1664 the port came under British rule and was renamed New York, but the story of Saint Nicholas, or Sinter Claes as the Dutch knew him, spread from the original immigrants along with the expectation that children would receive presents on the eve of 6 December. The present-giving antics of St Nicholas were later transferred to Christmas Eve (possibly because an end of November Thanksgiving celebration was too close to the present-giving of St Nicholas Eve). Sinter Claes was Anglicised as Santa Claus by the, then mostly English-speaking, inhabitants of New York.

By the early 19th century many American children expected Santa Claus to bring them presents at Christmas, but the custom only became a national one thanks to Professor Clement Clarke Moore. Born the son of a minister in 1779, he later became Professor of Oriental and Greek Literature at the General Theological Seminary in New York. In addition to his interest in the classical period he studied the folklore of Dutch, German and Scandinavian immigrants who had settled on the American east coast. In 1822 he wrote a poem that he later read to those who were staying with him over Christmas.

The poem might never have reached a wider audience had it not been copied by one of Moore's guests who later sent it to his local paper (the *Troy Sentinel*) where it was published anonymously on 23 December 1823. The poem quickly became a firm favourite and has since appeared in countless Christmas anthologies. It is widely understood to be the source of the modern-day image of Santa Claus. Indeed, many people believe that the descriptive passages in the poem refer specifically to Santa Claus, but it is St Nicholas, not Santa, who is mentioned by the devout Moore. The work is often published under an incorrect title, *The Night Before Christmas*, but was originally entitled *A Visit from St Nicholas*. At the time the poem was written Santa Claus was just a local synonym for St Nicholas. The poem, however, did not seem to be describing a typical St Nicholas, who was usually depicted as a tall, thin, sober man dressed in ecclesiastical garb and riding a flying horse.

A Visit from St Nicholas

Twas the night before Christmas, when all
through the house
Not a creature was stirring. Not even a mouse;
The stockings were hung by the chimney
with care,
In hopes that St Nicholas soon would be there;
The children were nestled all snug in their beds
While visions of sugar-plums danced in
their heads;
And mama in her kerchief, and I in my cap,
Had just settled our brains for a long
winter's nap,
When out on the lawn there arose such
a clatter,
I sprang from my bed to see what was
the matter.
Away to the window I flew like a flash,
Tore open the shutters and threw up the sash.
The moon on the breast of the new-fallen snow
Gave a lustre of midday to objects below;
When what to my wondering eyes
should appear,
But a miniature sleigh and eight tiny reindeer,
With a little old driver, so lively and quick,
I knew in a moment it must be St Nick.
More rapid than eagles his coursers they came,
And he whistled and shouted, and called them
by name:

'Now, Dasher! now, Dancer! now, Prancer
and Vixen!
On, Comet! on, Cupid! on, Donder and Blitzen!
To the top of the porch, to the top of the wall!
Now dash away, dash away, dash away, all!'
As dry leaves that before the wild hurricane fly,
When they meet with an obstacle, mount to
the sky,
So up to the housetop the coursers they flew,
With the sleigh full of toys, and St Nicholas
too.
And then in a twinkling I heard on the roof
The prancing and pawing of each little hoof.
As I drew in my head, and was turning around,
Down the chimney St Nicholas came with
a bound.
He was dressed all in fur from his head
to his foot,
And his clothes were all tarnished with ashes
and soot;
A bundle of toys he had slung on his back,
And he looked like a peddler just opening
a pack.
His eyes – how they twinkled! his dimples,
how merry!
His cheeks were like roses, his nose like
a cherry!
His droll little mouth was drawn up like a bow,
And the beard on his chin was as white as
the snow.

The stump of a pipe he held tight in his teeth.
And the smoke it encircled his head like
a wreath.
He had a broad face and a very round belly
That shook, when he laughed, like a bowl full
of jelly.
He was chubby and plump, a right jolly
old elf;
And I laughed when I saw him, in spite
of myself.
A wink of his eye and a twist of his head
Soon gave me to know I had nothing to dread.
He spoke not a word, but went straight to
his work,
And filled all the stockings; then turned with
a jerk,
And laying his finger aside of his nose,
And giving a nod, up the chimney he rose.
He sprang to his sleigh, to his team gave
a whistle,
And away they all flew like the down of a thistle;
But I heard him explain, ere he drove out of
sight,
'Happy Christmas to all, and to all a
good-night!'

The typical Christmas scene (as it would have been
in 19th-century New York) is provided by the image
of 'new-fallen snow' and the subject is referred to as
St Nick.

Notice that his visit has already been transferred from early December to Christmas Eve. Like St Nicholas, the white-bearded figure arrives in secret, at night and comes down the chimney bearing toys that he places in the children's stockings. A novel feature is his mode of transport (a miniature sleigh pulled by eight tiny reindeer) that, in common with the more traditional horse, flies

HE HAD A BROAD FACE AND A VERY ROUND BELLY THAT SHOOK, WHEN HE LAUGHED, LIKE A BOWL FULL OF JELLY. HE WAS CHUBBY AND PLUMP, A RIGHT JOLLY OLD ELF; AND I LAUGHED WHEN I SAW HIM, IN SPITE OF MYSELF.

through the air. Notice that there is no Rudolph among the reindeer names; he was to come later.

The most important part of the poem is the description of St Nick, who is dressed all in fur (the colour of his outfit is not revealed). *He* has a red nose (not the reindeer) and is smoking a pipe. Significantly, he is chubby and plump, with a very round belly and is described as 'a right jolly old elf'.

The smoking, jolly, elfish, fur-clad figure is a description that is a much closer fit with the shaman-based Dark Helper or even one of the north European gods of midwinter than with the typical St Nicholas figure. As has been previously pointed out, these pagan figures had already been merged with St Nicholas in a number of European countries. The fact that Professor Moore had studied the folklore of such countries may have accounted for his unusual St Nicholas and, as we will see later, is also a possible source of the substitution of the horse by eight reindeer.

There are, however, several other contemporary accounts of St Nicholas that may have been source material for Moore's poem. One of these was the widely read *Knickerbocker's History of New York* (1809) by Washington Irving, which included a humorous account of the Dutch Santa Claus legend. There was also a short poem in an 1821 issue of *The Children's Friend* that mentioned reindeer as Santa's mode of transport. To add to the controversy, recent research by Professor Don Foster concludes that the famous poem was not even written by Moore, who had an aversion to tobacco and was unlikely to have described a pipe-smoking saint. It also seems strange that the devout Moore makes no mention of the Nativity in the poem. Foster comes up with Henry Livingstone Jr, of Dutch descent, as the more likely author.

As it happens, the illustrations that have accompanied the poem have been even more important than the words in moulding the modern image of Santa. The earliest set of illustrations was by William Boyd in 1848, and showed St Nicholas as a strange-looking gentleman wearing a waistcoat, fur jacket and hat, smoking a short-stemmed pipe. It was, however, the drawings by Thomas Nast, published annually with the poem in the Christmas issues of *Harper's Weekly* from 1863, that were to come closer to the Santa of the 21st century. His earlier pictures were closer to Moore's description of a small, bearded elf and were more reminiscent of Germany's Dark Helper figure known as Pelz Nickel (fur-clad Nick). This is perhaps not surprising given that Nast was born in Bavaria. Other Nast illustrations showed Santa with a short rod, in place of his predecessor's broom, and a jack-in-the-box, a metaphor for copulation. Santa, like Father Christmas, was not without his sexual licence.

Nast's later pictures (the last one appeared in 1886) depicted a large, big-bellied, jovial, broad-faced man wearing boots and a furry suit, complete with a wide belt. On his head was either a pointed furry cap (some argue that this was derived from the mitre worn by St Nicholas) or a holly wreath, though the now very full-bearded figure was still often shown smoking a long-stemmed clay pipe. By then the poem and its illustrations had moved a long way from earlier images of St Nicholas. The Santa Claus figure had evolved via the rather frightening Dark Helper into a more friendly old-style, Bacchanalian Father Christmas figure. By 1891, President Harrison reported that he would be dressing up as Santa Claus at Christmas for the benefit of his grandchildren.

During the time of the Nast illustrations, the American Santa figure was exported to Victorian Britain. This was partly due to the success of English reprints of *The Christmas Stocking*, Susan Warner's American bestseller, originally published in 1854. As the Santa figure spread to England during the 1860s so too did the custom of giving presents at Christmas rather than at New Year. The British gift-bearer kept Father Christmas as a name and unlike his American model he wore a cloak and hood rather than a suit and cap. The famous Victorian illustrator Sir John Tenniel produced a more British version of Father Christmas.

Belief in Santa Claus rapidly became a part of childhood ritual and over the years adults, including clergymen and radio disc jockeys, have been castigated for declaring that Santa (or Father Christmas) does not exist. Some have argued that for clergymen to deny children their faith in the legendary figure of Father Christmas is no different to a denial of stories surrounding Jesus. As with the Tooth Fairy, some children have cherished their belief for longer than others and an example of this was famously aired in 1897 when the young Virginia O'Hanlon wrote to the editor of *The New York Sun*:

> I am eight years old. Some of my friends say
> there is no Santa Claus. Papa says,
> 'If you see it in THE SUN it's so'. Please tell me
> the truth, is there a Santa Claus?

Virginia's letter and the Editor's reply later appeared in the paper. His answer included the following:

> Virginia your friends are wrong. They have
> been affected by the skepticism (sic) of a
> skeptical age.

> Yes, Virginia there is a Santa Claus. He exists as
> certainly as love and generosity and devotion
> exist, and you know that they abound and give

to your life its highest beauty and joy! Alas! How dreary would the world be if there were no Santa Claus!

Not believe in Santa Claus? Nobody sees Santa Claus, but that is no sign that there is no Santa Claus.

No Santa Claus! Thank God he lives and lives forever. A thousand years from now, Virginia, nay, ten thousand years from now, he will continue to make glad the heart of childhood.

Virginia's letter and its reply were reprinted in the paper every December until the late 1940s when the paper folded. They still appear every year in *The New York Times*.

Santa (still referred to in Britain under his *alter ego* Father Christmas) has since become the central figure of Christmas in many parts of the world. In Britain the newly established St Nicholas Society is attempting to restrict the power of Santa and restore St Nicholas as a key symbol of the festive season. To this end there has been a recent increase in the number of church services featuring St Nicholas.

Did Coca-Cola Take Santa Over?

Following the introduction of Santa to Britain in the 1860s three important questions concerning the old gentleman remained to be answered. On page 124 we examine the first question, the issue of where Santa/Father Christmas spends the rest of the year when he is not actually delivering the presents. Dutch children may still believe that St Nicholas comes to them annually from his home in Spain, but the general view is that Santa's home is further north and suffers from a cold, snowy climate. The second question, How did reindeer became involved with Santa?, is explored on pages 104 to 112.

The remaining area of contention is the colour of Santa's furry suit. Thomas Nast's illustrations were in black and white, thus neatly avoiding any controversy. The Nast pictures were given colour by the artist Ted Menten in the late 20th century, when red was already the accepted colour. Unconfirmed reports record that another early illustrator of the Moore poem was a German called Moritz von Schwind who also showed Santa in a red costume.

In Britain the old Father Christmas figure was shown clad in clothes with a variety of colours, including blue, but forest green was the most common (see picture section). A green costume was also the hallmark of the Pan-like and Lord of Misrule figures of his ancestry. By the time of the American Santa import in Victorian times, the Christmas card was becoming popular, and early cards picturing Santa/Father Christmas can help us to trace the origin of his red and white costume. From these it appears that red starts to become popular in late Victorian times, an example being the card illustrated in the picture section that was first issued in 1889. By the early decades of the 20th century, red (with white trimmings) or green were the most common colours.

How then did red and white come to be the only accepted colour for Santa by the middle of the 20th century? In 1920s America the artist Norman Rockwell depicted Santa dressed in red in his festive pictures for the *Saturday Evening Post*. At about the same time in Britain one of our leading experts on European myth and folklore was beginning a series of pre-Christmas illustrated letters to his children. J. R. R. Tolkien sent the first of these letters, supposedly from Father Christmas, in 1920. Many of these have since been published in Tolkien's book *The Father Christmas Letters*. The colour illustrations show Father Christmas in a red, hooded cloak in most of his pictures, though for the 1936 letter he is shown with a separate red cap, red jacket and a pair of green trousers – possibly Tolkien hedging his bets.

Given that the Tolkien pictures were not exposed to a wider public gaze until after Santa's red and white suit became ubiquitous, we need to look elsewhere to find the illustrator who was to help tip the balance in favour of a red and white livery for Santa. The illustrations of Santa produced by the Swedish artist Haddon Sundblom were of a rather more commercial nature than those created by Boyd, Nast or Tolkien, in that they were designed as advertisements for Coca-Cola.

The first of Sundblom's Santas appeared only in the States, in 1931, and featured a jolly Santa in a red tunic with white cuffs. Santa is shown holding not his traditional pipe but a glass of Coca-Cola. Behind him is the Coca-Cola sign with the letters picked out in white on a red background: the company's colours. Unusually, Santa is without any head covering, but this is explained by the legend 'My hat's off to the pause that refreshes'. By the 1930s the company had altered its recipe (it is alleged that it originally contained coca leaves) but it was still not allowed to advertise Coca-Cola as a drink for children. The Sundblom Santa advert neatly sidestepped this ban and also encouraged people to drink Coca-Cola during the winter.

BRITAIN IS NOW LEFT WITH THE AMERICAN VERSION OF SANTA, INCLUDING SUIT, BELT AND HAT RATHER THAN THE EARLIER BRITISH CLOAKED FIGURE. SANTA ALSO DID A LOT FOR COCA-COLA.

Sundblom produced a whole series of illustrations for Coca-Cola's annual Christmas advertising campaign and all showed Santa dressed in red, with a white shirt or jacket cuffs. Santa is shown in the typical American style with separate trousers and jacket. He is usually depicted with a pointed red cap (with white brim) and a broad buckled belt. The international marketing based on Santa with his Coke ran for over 30 years and included references to GIs in 1941. Sundblom's last 'Coca-Cola Santa' appeared in 1964.

Although Sundblom was not the first artist to show Santa dressed in red and white, his Coca-Cola campaign certainly had an enormous impact on the international image of Santa Claus. Not only have alternative colours faded away but Britain (and the rest of the world) is now left with the American version of Santa, including suit, belt and hat rather than the earlier British cloaked figure. Santa also did a lot for Coca-Cola.

There are traditionalists who seek a religious link behind the colour of Santa's suit. Some have argued that St Nicholas should indeed be shown wearing a red cloak on his feast day (6 December) as the liturgical colour for Advent is red. There may actually be a more deep-rooted reason for the red and white colours, but to understand this requires a trip back in time to stories of yet another pagan precursor of Santa.

Santa and his Magic Mushrooms

Coca-Cola may have focused attention on Santa's red costume but there is another, much more ancient story that not only helps to explain his red and white clothing but also his reindeer transport, affinity with chimneys and more importantly his state of mind. As to the latter, it is frequently hinted (if only in his flushed face and repeated 'Ho-Ho') that the flying Santa has imbibed something rather stronger than Coca-Cola. Most people assume this to be alcohol but there is a much more interesting, alternative explanation.

For the majority of north Europeans shamans remain, at most, a very distant part of folk memory.

The same cannot be said in much of Lapland, that part of Europe that is mostly above the Arctic Circle and comprises parts of Sweden, Norway, Finland and Russia. Shamanism also survived well into the 20th century in parts of Siberia (the Asiatic part of Russia). These regions, most of which border on the Arctic Ocean, have been home to tribes of nomadic reindeer hunters for thousands of years. For many of these groups alcohol played little or no part in their lives until spirits such as vodka were introduced in the 19th and 20th centuries.

Reasons for the former lack of alcohol in these areas include the extreme cold (yeast needs warmth to convert sugars to alcohol) and the drawback of having to transport a heavy commodity such as alcohol each time a tribe moved on to follow their reindeer herds. Despite the absence of alcohol, these northern reindeer herders had at least one other means of inebriation. For over 300 years, visitors to Siberia and neighbouring regions recorded instances of both recreational and ritualistic use of a red and white mushroom known in the West as the fly agaric (*Amanita muscaria*). Most records come from the Siberian Samoyed, Koryak, Chukchi and Kamchadel tribes, but the Saami and other reindeer-herding peoples who have long roamed Lapland also have an extensive history of eating fly agaric.

To the Koryaks the fly agaric was believed to have sprung from the spittle of their ancient god Vahiyinen. The fungus's magic powers are more distantly remembered in parts of the old Yugoslavia. Here legend recounts that one night in late December, Wotan (also known as Odin, one of St Nicholas's forerunners) was journeying through the sky on his horse Sleipner when he was chased by evil demons. As the horse galloped ever faster, blood-flecked foam from his lips spattered the ground and turned into fly agaric mushrooms.

To most more southern-based Europeans the fly agaric has long been regarded as highly toxic. Though some of the chemicals can indeed cause digestive upset and symptoms of ill health, others produce a hallucinogenic effect. It was for this reason that the fly agaric was consumed in Siberia and Lapland, both as part of rituals and in a manner comparable to the recreational use of alcohol.

Early European visitors noted that the fungus was carefully dried before being ingested, and that this not only preserved the specimens but also reduced the likelihood of poisonous side effects. The limited seasonal and numerical availability of fly agaric may have given rise to the custom (found in both Siberia and Lapland) that involved drinking the urine of someone who had recently eaten fly agaric. The result of this is that the urine drinker also becomes intoxicated, although the effect of the urine is weaker than that of the mushroom.

The Saami people even fed fly agarics to their reindeer and then drank the reindeers' urine. Mushroom eaters would also often drink their own urine so as to prolong the period of hallucination. Such people were described as 'being be-mushroomed' or more interestingly as 'getting pissed' – a phrase that has since passed into the European culture of alcoholic overindulgence (especially at Christmas) but may well pre-date the invention of alcohol.

Over 100 years ago, an alkaloid chemical christened muscarine was isolated from fly agaric and was at first believed to be the main poisonous agent. Although it may be responsible for the twitching exhibited by those intoxicated by the fungus, it is normally present in amounts too small to produce the more serious (even fatal) symptoms associated with fungi containing large amounts of muscarine. Fly agaric also contains small amounts of the alkaloid bufotenine, a chemical found in toads (frequently used in hallucinogenic preparations). This may be why the fungus is often referred to as a toadstool. For more information on the fly agaric see *How to Identify Edible Mushrooms*.

The two most important chemicals found in fly agaric are ibotenic acid and muscimol. These produce the main symptoms exhibited by those who ingest the mushroom. Ibotenic acid is the less stable compound but is converted to muscimol when the mushroom dries or is gently heated. Thus the custom of eating the dried fungus ensured a greater amount of the more stable hallucinogen, resulting in a more potent product. Researchers have shown that hallucinogenic muscimol passes largely unaltered into the urine of both man and reindeer, but the more dangerous muscarine is broken down in the kidneys. This means that 'getting pissed' may be safer than eating the fungus.

These northern peoples used to derive their meat, milk, clothing, footwear, ornaments and mode of transport from the nomadic reindeer that they had semi-domesticated. In addition, the covering of the tent-like, easily transported, summer yurts was made from reindeer hide. Reindeer are also known to become intoxicated after eating fly agaric. Members of an 18th-century expedition to eastern Siberia came upon a reindeer staggering around in a stupor. Having killed and eaten the animal, the diners also became intoxicated.

In Lapland the Saami herders still occasionally use the smell of dried fly agaric as an aid when rounding up reindeer. Reindeer have even been seen licking patches of man-made yellow snow. This may be because of the salt content in urine, but perhaps they too enjoy 'getting pissed'. An early 20th-century traveller to Siberia remarked, 'The position of a man standing in the open while urinating is rather critical when he becomes the object of attention from reindeer coming down on him at full speed.'

It was, however, the ritualistic use of fly agaric by the tribal shaman that was much more significant than its recreational use. This was especially true when used in response to the need for a cure by a sick or injured member of the group. The hallucinogenic fly agaric was employed by the tribal shaman (the term comes from the Siberian word *saman*) to obtain a trance-like state. Under the influence of the fungus (and drum rhythms) shamans were said to travel to the heavens (a feeling as of 'flying'), where they gained strength and knowledge with which to help their people.

The Siberian winter dwellings were more substantial than the portable summer yurts, and most had only one entrance that also served as the smoke hole. As a result, visitors such as the shaman would enter via the equivalent of our chimney. Significantly, early Siberian poetry includes accounts of people writing messages to their gods which were then burnt; the belief being that their request travelled to the gods via the smoke hole. These traditions pre-date the more recent Western custom of putting messages for Santa up the chimney. In parts of Germany the symbol of chimney sweeps is the fly agaric and sweeps are considered symbols of luck for the New Year.

THE SIBERIAN WINTER DWELLINGS HAD ONLY ONE ENTRANCE THAT ALSO SERVED AS THE SMOKE HOLE. VISITORS SUCH AS THE SHAMAN WOULD ENTER VIA THE EQUIVALENT OF OUR CHIMNEY.

Midwinter was a very busy time for the shaman, not least because in such northern regions the sun does not rise above the horizon for over a month either side of the winter solstice. Depression, or winter blues (now known as seasonal affective disorder or SAD) and extreme cold would result in more illness than usual. So around our Christmas time much use would be made of the red and white-spotted fly agaric. The euphoric, be-mushroomed shaman, dressed in reindeer furs, often sporting reindeer antlers and having 'flown' to the heavens to gain knowledge from the gods, would come down the chimney bringing gifts of healing.

Today in Germany the fly agaric is, like the sweep, still looked on as a symbol of good luck and in many parts of central Europe its image regularly appears on Christmas cards and as Christmas tree decorations, a custom that has recently spread to Britain.

The following poem first appeared in the *British Journal of General Practice*, December 2000:

A Christmas Gift from Siberia

For Tony and Patrick

Santa lays his hand
on my head, and yours
a shaman
with gifts of healing
from worlds
the other side of the mushroom.

Rudolph carried him,
his nose as red as the scarlet fungus
with white spots
he shared with his master
to fly to the lands of wisdom

Come into my house
where we huddle for warmth underground;
there's no need to knock

at my open door in the roof
where the smoke drifts out
from the fire.

Welcome Santa
brave traveller,
healer.

(Gillie Bolton)

It is more than likely that Professor Clement Moore knew of the Lapland fly agaric customs outlined above, given his interest in north European folklore. If so, this could have influenced his description of St Nicholas and especially his use of reindeer. It is unlikely that Moore had ever seen a sleigh pulled by reindeer, though some argue that the reindeer idea came from the American continent, specifically the Inuit of Alaska and Canada. Here, however, the animals are known as caribou and such people use dogs, not reindeer, as draught animals. As we shall see, it is the land of the Saami peoples of Lapland, with their knowledge of reindeer and fly agaric, that now draws many winter visitors in search of the Santa experience.

An account of the Siberian custom of eating fly agaric was published in Mordecei Cooke's popular British book *A Plain and Easy Account of British Fungi*. The book, first published in 1862, included a detailed list of the effects produced by eating the fungus was the sensation that objects increase in size:

Erroneous impressions of size and distance are common occurrences: a straw lying in the road becomes a formidable object, to overcome which a leap is taken sufficient to clear a barrel of ale …

Mordecei was a contemporary of the Revd Charles Dodgson, who is said to have read a review of the book (and maybe the book itself). It is perhaps no coincidence that in the same year that Mordecei's book was published, Dodgson began work on a story provisionally entitled *Alice's Adventures Under Ground*. The work was finally published in 1865 as *Alice's Adventures in Wonderland*, under Dodgson's pseudonym of Lewis Carroll. The perception of things (or people) out of scale, a common result of the ingestion of fly agaric, features strongly in the book:

There was a large mushroom growing near her, about the same height as herself … And her eyes immediately met those of a large blue caterpillar, that was sitting on the top with its arms folded, quietly smoking a long hookah …

'Are you content now?' said the Caterpillar.

'Well I should like to be a little larger, sir, if you wouldn't mind,' said Alice.

'One side will make you grow taller, and the other will make you grow shorter.'

'One side of what? The other side of what?' thought Alice to herself.

'Of the mushroom,' said the caterpillar, just as if she had asked it aloud ...

After a while she remembered that she still held the pieces of mushrooms in her hands, and she set to work very carefully, nibbling first one and then at the other, and growing sometimes taller and sometimes shorter, until she had succeeded in bringing herself down to her usual height.

Just as the illustrations to Moore's Christmas poem have influenced successive generations so those by Sir John Tenniel in the first edition of *Alice's Adventures in Wonderland* are justly famous. It is worth noting that in a letter concerning the book's binding, sent by Dodgson to his publishers in 1864, he wrote: 'I have been considering the question of the colour of *Alice's Adventures*, and have come to the conclusion that bright red will be the best ...'

It is perhaps appropriate that Dodgson's only trip abroad took him to Russia, though the closest he would have come to people consuming fly agaric was the urban environment of St Petersburg. Over the years *Alice* has been a popular Christmas present and also the basis of pantomime and other Christmas dramatic productions. As with so many aspects of our modern Christmas it originated in Victorian times; indeed, Dodgson presented a copy of the book to Princess Beatrice, the eight-year-old daughter of Queen Victoria. Just as the red and white fly agaric may have been behind much of the imagery of our modern Santa, so the dreamlike state of Alice's adventures and her frequent apparent changes in size can be laid at the door of this archetypal toadstool.

Rudolph and the Rest

Rudolph was not one of the eight named reindeer in Clement Moore's poem (page 93). He first appeared in a short story written by Robert L. May in 1939. The story was used to promote the American department store for which Mr May worked. The name Rudolph is said to have originated with his young daughter. The song 'Rudolph the Red-nosed Reindeer' was written by May's brother-in-law, Johny Marks, and first hit the big time sung by Gene Autry in 1949.

If urine drinking is one of the less well-known habits of Santa's sleigh bearers, other facts are now better known, especially since the research of Caroline Pond in the 1980s. Scientifically, the species is known as *Rangifer tarandus* and this includes various subspecies that range over parts of northern Europe, Eurasia and North America. Reindeer (or caribou) are superbly adapted to life in snowy, barren areas. Their broad, splayed hooves act like snow-shoes, preventing them from sinking into deep snow, and also help them to dig away snow in search of food. Special bones in the feet produce a clicking sound that acts as a form of communication between members of a herd. Reindeer fur is a very efficient insulator with long, hollow hairs supporting a dense underfur (over 300 hairs to the square cm) that traps warm air around the body, resulting in a duvet-like snugness.

The famous nose contains a block of much-folded bone covered with blood-rich membranes; these warm the air as the animal breathes in and cool it as it breathes out. As a result, both heat and water are conserved even at temperatures as low as -60 C. A red nose in a reindeer is most likely to be the result of a parasitic infection, though Rudolph's problem is usually put down to a winter cold (most unlikely) or a drop of alcohol, something a little closer to the truth – see below. Reindeer are rather like seals in that they are curious of people, often approaching them and sniffing, so it is perhaps not such a surprise that they developed a taste for human urine.

In winter reindeer live mainly on lichens, mosses and low-growing plants which they reach after digging (or using their antlers) to remove the snow. Contrary to popular belief they do not like the weather to be as that in the Good King Wenceslas carol, 'when the snow lay round about, deep and crisp and even'. Too deep and the plants cannot be reached, too crisp makes the snow too hard to dig through. Special gut bacteria enable reindeer to extract maximum nourishment from their poor diet and the bacteria even produce small quantities of alcohol – so Siberian reindeer experienced alcohol long before their minders. Animals fatten up during the summer and autumn and, in Lapland at least, they eat very little over Christmas – in marked contrast to many humans.

Perhaps the biggest misconception of the Santa story is that his sleigh is pulled by eight strapping male reindeer, all sporting magnificent antlers. As it happens the reindeer is the only species of deer in which both males and females develop antlers. Females keep their antlers until at least late spring, having used them to reach food under the snow and to fend off predators from their young. Males are more typical in that they use their antlers in fights with other males as they bid for the best females. By midwinter most males are not only too tired to pull a laden sleigh but they will also have shed their antlers. The eight strapping antler-clad beasts shown pulling St Nicholas through the sky at Christmas must therefore be female. It appears that as usual it is the women that do most of the work at Christmas.

BY MIDWINTER MOST MALES ARE NOT ONLY TOO TIRED TO PULL A LADEN SLEIGH BUT THEY WILL ALSO HAVE SHED THEIR ANTLERS.

The Laps get round the problem of energy loss in male reindeer by using castrated males (which keep their antlers much longer than the bulls) to pull their sleighs and indeed for the popular modern sport of reindeer racing. Reindeer also feature in *Father Christmas*, the popular cartoon book by Raymond Briggs. His pictures are based rather more closely on our own roe deer – he thought they looked more able to fly. In fact reindeer are surprisingly small, except for the antlers that seem too large for their body size.

For most of the year the nearest that British children can get to a herd of semi-wild reindeer is in Scotland. Alan and Tilly Smith run the Reindeer Centre from Glenmore at the foot of the Cairngorms. The herd size exceeds 150 animals and they roam over some 6,000 acres. Reindeer became extinct in Scotland about 6000 BC but were reintroduced from Lapland in the early 1950s by a Saami called Mikel Utsi. When the project was started the idea was to promote reindeer meat as an alternative to the usual Christmas flesh, but the thought of feasting on an animal so closely associated with Father Christmas proved unacceptable to the British public.

In December some of the Scottish animals (geldings that do not lose their antlers until after Christmas) often take part in Father Christmas events at Harrods and in shopping centres around the country. Sadly, in 2001, their movement outside Scotland was banned owing to concerns that they might spread foot and mouth disease. A greater tragedy hit many of the reindeer herders of Lapland in 1986, when radiation from the leaking nuclear reactor at Chernobyl rendered reindeer meat unfit for human consumption.

Letters and Father Christmas Online

Whether they are derived from messages sent to the gods via the smoke hole (page 109) or requests to St Nicholas lodged in the chimney, the idea of sending letters to Father Christmas has been around for many years. Between them, Santa and Father Christmas get more letters than anyone else in the world, but they are sent to a range of different addresses.

If the image of the modern present-giver originated with Moore's poem in 1823, then the spirit of giving in Britain was further promoted in 1843, with the publication of *A Christmas Carol*. Not many years later, children began to leave messages for the present-giver. We have already seen (page 97) how the illustrator Thomas Nast influenced our view of Santa but he also created a new tradition when, in 1863, he drew Santa reading a letter sent to him from a child. In both Britain and America, letters from children detailing present requests rapidly caught on as a new Christmas custom.

Not long after this, people began to compose imaginary letters back to children, as in this extract from a letter sent by Mark Twain:

> Palace of St Nicholas
> In the Moon
> Christmas Morning
>
> Dear Susie Clemens
>
> I have received and read all of the letters which you and your little sister have written me ... I went down your chimney at midnight when you were asleep ...

In 1996 a letter destined for Santa came to light when a bedroom chimney was being cleaned as part of a cottage renovation in Wiltshire. The letter, written in copperplate handwriting on four pages of an exercise book, was dated 8 December 1911, and was written by a nine-year-old girl called Mabel Higgs.

> Dear Santa Claus
> Last year you brought me many nice presents and I think you were very kind indeed. I expect you would like to know what I should like you to bring me this year. Well, I should like you to bring me a storybook, a postcard album, a box of chocolates and a sweetshop.
> We have a little baby and we would like you to bring her a rattle that will blow.
> I hope you will remember the very poor children in the slums and in the large towns.
> I might stay awake for some time to see you come in our bedroom to put the things in my stocking the night you come. Our house is on the common.
>
> With much love, I remain your little friend, Mabel.

Mabel's daughter was shown the letter and commented that the letter was in keeping with the way her mum had been as an adult. Only a few years after the letter was written, children asked not only for presents but also for the safe return of their father (or other family members) from the Great War.

Between the wars a family of four children living in Oxford left letters for Father Christmas by the fireplace in a manner similar to that of many others. What was unusual was that the Tolkien children also received a letter each year, just before Christmas. The first of these arrived in 1920 when John, the eldest child, was three. The letters continued to arrive for some 20 years, as the children grew up. The letters were addressed from the North Pole, written in spidery writing and signed Father Christmas or Father Nicholas Christmas. They were written by their father J. R. R. Tolkien who, as author of the *Lord of the Rings*, had an extensive knowledge of folklore. As such he would have been well aware of the St Nicholas model for Santa, but still preferred to use the English name Father Christmas.

Later published as *The Father Christmas Letters*, they tell of the exploits of Father Christmas and his chief assistant the North Polar Bear. Elves also feature, as do Red Gnomes and Goblins, the latter causing lots of problems. Some of the letters mention his reindeer and the importing of new young ones from Lapland. There are also messages to the children, as for example in 1925, when he enquired of Michael as to when he was going to be able to read and write his own letters to Father Christmas.

Tolkien's letters of the 1920s and 1930s all purportedly came from Father Christmas's home at the North Pole. For American children there was a different destination for letters addressed to Santa. On Christmas Eve in 1852, German settlers named their new Indiana town Santa Claus and, following a 1920 magazine article about the town, children began sending their Santa letters there. A local resident began sending replies, a custom later continued by his daughter.

Every year British children address many thousands of letters to Father Christmas. For the past 40 years these have been processed by the Royal Mail (Consignia) at a depot (Reindeer Land) outside Belfast. Those writers who post early enough and include a name and address receive a standard reply – by the end of the 1990s this involved some 750,000 letters each year. An example, as **DESPITE THE VIEW THAT CHILDREN NOW EXPECT EVER MORE EXPENSIVE PRESENTS, MANY OF THE LETTERS SENT BY CHILDREN INCLUDE A PLEA TO FATHER CHRISTMAS FOR WORLD PEACE.** received by my son Martin, is shown on pages 122 and 123. Despite the view that children now expect ever more expensive presents, many of the letters sent by children include a plea to Father Christmas for world peace (this was especially so in 2001 after the Twin Towers attack). Others ask for the reunion of separated parents or work for unemployed family members.

In the last few years some children have taken to sending e-mails rather than letters to Father Christmas. It remains to be seen whether the traditional letter will survive under the onslaught of new technology and a shake-up in the postal services. For those wishing to keep up with Santa on Christmas Eve when he sets off to deliver his presents round the world, the website (http://www.noradsanta.org) depicts him working his way through the time zones, but interestingly shows his initial take-off point to be the North Pole. This is by no means his sole address ...

Where Does Father Christmas Live?

The first chance for children to see Father Christmas in his grotto was during 1888, in London, when the custom was started by Roberts department store. By the middle of the 20th century, grottos were commonplace and Santa even visited schools. In 1985 one Santa was

ROYAL MAIL
POSTAGE PAID
1
REINDEER LAND

Martin Harding
36 Marshall Road.
SHEFFIELD
S8 0GN

01963

The Royal Mail is delighted to help Father Christmas deliver his cards.

Santa's Grotto,
Reindeerland.
SAN TA1

My dear friend,

Many thanks for your super letter. I've had so many this year. It's great to hear from you all, I've been rushed off my feet. So I've only just found time to take my boots off, sit down and write back to you.

Of course, I've been busy making lots and lots of toys. Luckily I've got helpers – elves and reindeers – and we're all now busy putting up our Christmas decorations.

All the toys are packed, ready to deliver. I'll be doing that late on Christmas Eve, so don't worry and don't wait up. I'll drop the presents in when you're asleep

Until then, bags of love

father Christmas xxx

**LETTERS FROM FATHER CHRISTMAS SENT TO THE
AUTHOR'S SON MARTIN**

reputedly sacked from his grotto after giving a child a toy gun and telling him to 'Take that and shoot Margaret Thatcher'. By the start of the 21st century the craze for grottos was on the decline and fewer stores were installing a December Santa.

For those wishing to visit the man in his 'real' home there are a number of options. It was in 1869 that the North Pole was first suggested as the home base for Father Christmas, in a poem by George Webster. This is in keeping with Scandinavian traditions and the North Pole was also the address of Tolkien's collection of *Father Christmas Letters*.

The power of Walt Disney was to change things when, in the 1933 film *Santa's Workshop*, Donald Duck visited Santa in Nuuk, the capital of Greenland. This southern shift introduced Santa to a slightly more accessible part of the world and one that (unlike the North Pole) was a true home to reindeer. The film

IT WAS IN 1869 THAT THE NORTH POLE WAS FIRST SUGGESTED AS THE HOME BASE FOR FATHER CHRISTMAS.

resulted in thousands of letters addressed to Santa in Greenland. The fact that the writers received a reply helped to fuel a lucrative December tourist trade.

It was entertainment of a more local sort that helped to move Santa's home a little further to the east. In the 1920s a popular Finnish radio personality ('Uncle Marcus') featured in a broadcast depicting Santa at his home on 'Ear Mountain' in northern Finland. This story has since been used by the Lappish Tourist Board to promote Finland as Santa's home. The organisation has helped to develop the area around Rovaniemi (the Arctic capital of Finnish Lapland) as a centre for tourists seeking the Santa experience.

In 1996, £100,000 of European Union funds was utilised to improve the facilities at Rovaniemi. Santa Claus village is just a few miles from the airport and includes his 'Official Post Office', now handling over 750,000 letters sent to Santa each festive season (the greatest number comes from Japan). Santa-endorsed Coca-Cola machines are much in evidence and snowmobiles take people to inspect the reindeer and partake in mock shamanic rituals in local 'wigwams'. Inside the aptly named SantaPark, housed in an artificial cavern originally constructed as a nuclear shelter, visitors can even eat reindeer. Naturally the experience includes a visit to Santa. Nowhere is there any mention of the Nativity.

Other Santa sites include two in Iceland, one at Drobak, near Oslo, and a revitalised site in Greenland that is staging a fightback against Lapland. At Nuuk there is a Rudolph the Red-Nosed Reindeer Restaurant and a recently developed Santa Claus Workshop. Sleigh rides are included in the attractions. The post office there processes those letters sent to Father Christmas, The North Pole, Greenland. Greenland even boasts a Santa castle, in the form of a sod hut made for a Danish television programme. Canada runs Santa centres and he also has a workshop in the town of North Pole, Colorado. Santa gets around.

Several cities further to the south host Christmas markets in the run-up to Christmas. Many of these were begun when St Nicholas was the central present-giving figure. One example in Munich dates back to the 14th century, when it was known as the Nicholas Market. The present-day Christkindlmarkt in the central square consists of many stalls selling Christmas decorations and other crafts. Chestnuts are roasted, ginger biscuits baked and *gluhwein* (hot spiced wine) is consumed in large quantities while both Santa and more traditional, mitre-clad St Nicholas figures dispense sweets to children. As for St Nicholas, his hometown in Turkey does a roaring trade in Santa mementoes as well as more religious souvenirs.

In Britain, places such as Lincoln hold pre-Christmas street markets and many people travel to Bethlehem in Wales (Carmarthenshire) during December, if only to get the coveted frank for their Christmas cards. Sadly the tiny village no longer supports an official post office but the owner of the former post office retains the right to frank the village name on letters as long as he uses *Llythyrdy*, the Welsh word for post office, above the door.

There is no chance of being turned away from the inn as the Welsh Bethlehem does not possess one, but it is only a matter of time before someone comes up with the idea of a theme park nearby.

CHRISTMAS CUSTOMS

The Yule Log and the Tree of Fire

'What is a Yule log?' I ask the class when I help out at my daughter's primary school in the run-up to Christmas.

'It's a chocolate Swiss roll with holly on the top,' comes the reply.

In fairness to the children, Sheffield has been a smokeless zone since the 1950s, and elsewhere in Britain most modern houses either lack an open fire, or lack one of sufficient grate-size for a real Yule log.

The significance of the winter solstice celebrations to the people of the Middle East and the more southern parts of Europe has been discussed earlier. In the colder, darker areas of northern Europe the winter solstice was an even more auspicious occasion and, as with the bonfires heralding the summer solstice, fire played a principal role in the festivities. The harshness of the winter climate meant that, in contrast to the communal outdoor summer bonfires, the winter blazes were held indoors and thus became more family oriented.

Fire was a feature of both the north European solstice celebrations and the southern ceremonies with their burning of fires and lamps to the sun-god on 25 December, and this theme continues today with the burning of candles at Christmas. So what is behind it? Tony van Renterghem is interested in the close link between the importance of fire in many myths and customs, and the origin of the making of fire by human beings.

CHILDREN BRINGING IN THE YULE LOG (1940s)

Old Father Christmas   1889

1889 Christmas card depicting Old Father Christmas
dressed in red and white.

Top: Late 19th Century card showing Santa dressed in blue.

Bottom: 19th Century card with a besom holding Santa dressed in green.

THE GLASTONBURY THORN

Joseph of Arimathea and the Glastonbury Thorn. Many believe that Joseph came to Britain carrying a staff made from a hawthorn from Christ's crown of thorns. He stuck his staff in the ground and the plant took root.

Top: *Amanita muscaria* – the hallucinogenic fly agaric mushroom.

Bottom: The red bracts and tiny flowers of poinsettia.

It seems likely that our first source of fire was from lightning strikes, especially where these set fire to vegetation. A tree not only burns for a long time, but the carrying of its burning branches would provide the means of lighting fires for warmth, protection and cooking. It was probably some time before we learnt how to make fire and, given the infrequency of lightning, this meant that once lit it would be important to keep a fire burning for as long as possible. Much later, even though they were able to make fire, the Romans kept an eternal fire, watched over by the vestal virgins. Eternal flames and slow-burning candles are still a feature of many modern faiths.

The story of our first use of fire is told in myth and legend from many countries. Common to most of these is the belief that fire belonged to the gods and that, in stealing fire, we would suffer unless we appeased the gods. The Ancient Greeks believed that Prometheus had stolen fire from the heavens, whilst Norse (Scandinavian) myths name Loki and the snake of lightning as the culprits. With fire it was felt that we acquired the knowledge of how to control nature, something about which the gods would not have been pleased. There is an obvious link here with the biblical story where the snake tempts Eve with the fruit of the tree of knowledge. The knowledge acquired from the tree puts Adam and Eve above the ignorant (and innocent) animal state and as punishment for stealing it they are expelled from the earthly paradise.

As an appeasement to the gods and in a symbolic

attempt to return the gift of fire, many communities made 'sacrifices' in the form of burning trees. The fires were mostly lit at important dates including the start of a New Year (often at or close to the winter solstice). While the custom originally involved burning an entire tree, the Nordic-Germanic midwinter celebrations centred on appeasing the god Thor by burning a branch known as the Yule log. Yule comes from *juleiss*, the Gothic name for December, a month much given to celebrations. The Old Norse word was *jól*, a form of which still exists in the Dutch language as joel or jól, meaning loud partying. Wishing someone a 'Jolly Christmas' fuses pagan and Christian values.

Many of the fire ceremonies (especially during some of the autumn/harvest festivals), which included sacrifices of animal or human effigies, may also have originated from a Norse myth, according to J. G. Frazer. In the story (about mistletoe) that is told on page 134 the body of the god Balder is burnt on a funeral pyre.

Winter solstice fires were also an attempt to 'strengthen the sun' as its intensity reached its nadir towards the end of December. In the most northern parts of Europe the amount of daylight around the time of midwinter is minimal (or even non-existent) and this time often coincides with a period of intensely cold weather. Both the light and warmth from the Yule fires would have helped those from more northern countries overcome the physical and mental hardships of winter.

Even in Britain the short days and dearth of sunshine

can influence people's mood. In recent years psychiatrists have discovered that SAD (seasonal affective disorder) is associated with the effect of light on the production of serotonin, a nerve transmitter in the brain that can influence mood. Perhaps the midwinter fires and lights were a precursor of the modern bank of strip lights used to alleviate these winter blues.

The Yule log tradition probably travelled from Scandinavia to Britain with the Vikings and has much in common with customs long practised in parts of Germany and France. In Britain, Celtic customs that would have pre-dated any Viking imports placed great significance on the oak tree, as this was sacred to their spiritual leaders, the Druids. The Druids' winter solstice fire was part of the maintenance of perpetual fire from which people re-lit their winter fires. As oak is slow burning it fulfilled the role well. The Yule log tradition was later incorporated into the Christian Christmas celebrations. Accounts mention that it was normally 'lit on Christmas Eve and burned through the 12 nights of Christmas until Twelfth Night'. There are still a number of places, including old inns, where this tradition is maintained.

EMBERS FROM THE YULE LOG WERE OFTEN KEPT IN A HOUSE THROUGHOUT THE YEAR AS A TALISMAN TO PROTECT THE HOUSE FROM FIRE AND LIGHTNING.

Embers from the Yule log were often kept in a house throughout the year as a talisman to protect the house from fire and lightning. This relates back to the tree of fire myth outlined earlier. Ashes from the Yule fire were frequently scattered as a fertiliser on the fields. This is probably a hangover from ancient fertility rites associated with midwinter fires, but wood ash does contain useful quantities of plant nutrients, including potash.

Mistletoe Kissing and Asterix's Magic Potion

Mistletoe or *Viscum album*, to give the plant its Latin name, is still frequently portrayed on Christmas cards and is readily available in greengrocers and supermarkets in the run-up to Christmas. Its popularity as a Christmas decoration, however, has diminished sharply in the past 40 years, the victim of an age of greater sexual freedom and political correctness. A report in the *Guardian* in December 1972 quoted a trader: 'It's a different sort of age. When they strip off naked in Leicester Square you can see why they don't need mistletoe today.'

In contrast to the long-term use of holly and ivy it is only relatively recently that mistletoe has become an accepted part of Christmas decorations in churches. In 1958 the *Daily Mirror* carried the headline 'Mistletoe has been Banned from a Church this Christmas', with the vicar describing it as 'a pagan decoration'. It further revealed that the vicar of St Thomas's Church, Derby, had nothing against mistletoe in the home and commented, 'I enjoy kissing pretty girls under it as much as anyone else.'

The roles played by mistletoe in pagan myth are many, and largely result from its unusual habitat (as a partial parasite growing on trees, it makes no contact with the ground) and its odd growth form. Notable features of mistletoe include its strangely forked stems, separate male and female plants, and the midwinter production of its frequently paired, spherical fruits set against a background of evergreen leaves. These have all helped to elevate mistletoe to the status of a sacred plant and have provided the source material for many legends.

In stories recalled in the previous section (the Yule log and the tree of fire), both oak and lightning were important components. An associated part of one story was the widely held belief that mistletoe grew spontaneously on trees (especially oak) that had been struck by lightning. The zig-zag nature of mistletoe stems has been likened to fork lightning and in many parts of Europe mistletoe has long been used as a talisman to protect houses from lightning and fire in a manner comparable to the use of the Yule log's embers.

The evergreen nature of the plant, as with holly and ivy, is regarded as being symbolic of the eternal life of Jesus and an excuse for its inclusion in the Christmas decorations. In earlier pagan times evergreens gave people hope that the sun had not died but would rise again after the winter solstice. The golden-yellow colour of mistletoe and its spherical growth form were even compared with the sun and gave rise to the classical myth of the 'Golden Bough' picked by Aeneas from an oak tree at the entrance to the underworld.

Mistletoe also features prominently in the story of the death of Balder, one of the great Norse legends. Balder was the beautiful, wise son of the great god Odin. He dreamed about his own death and on being told of this his mother, the goddess Frigg, made all things on Earth swear that they would not harm Balder. Following this, the other gods amused themselves by making fruitless efforts to kill the seemingly invincible Balder.

The god Loki was jealous of Balder and wished him dead. Loki disguised himself as an old woman and learnt from Frigg that mistletoe had been deemed too young and weak to harm Balder and had not been required to swear the oath. On hearing this, Loki sharpened the end of a mistletoe twig and presented it to the blind god Hother as an arrow to shoot at Balder as part of the light-hearted goading of his apparent invincibility. The mistletoe arrow pierced and killed Balder. His body was then taken to his ship where it was burnt on a great fire (along with his wife and horse). In revenge his grieving mother is said to have banished mistletoe to the tops of trees.

It is interesting to compare the above legend with one circulating in the Middle Ages, describing the wood of the cross (*lignum crucis*) on which Jesus was crucified as coming not from one of the common Middle-Eastern trees such as olive but from mistletoe.

It was even believed that mistletoe had been a large tree until the crucifixion when it had shrunk in shame and been denied all contact with the ground. Mistletoe's Old French name *herbe de la croix* is a reminder of this story.

The powerful magic of mistletoe has also long been part of the Celtic traditions that originated in Gaul where the plant is still abundant. In the 1st century AD, the Roman philosopher Pliny wrote about the Celtic Druids and their veneration of the oak. He reported their belief that anything (but especially mistletoe), growing on oak was sent from heaven and therefore imbued with healing powers. The production of a mistletoe potion involved collecting it from an oak tree on a certain day of the moon's cycle (the first day of their month) by cutting it with a golden sickle (iron and other base metals supposedly destroyed the magic).

The harvested plant was caught in a white cloth and thus not allowed to touch the ground. Among the 'all-heal' properties of mistletoe was its use as a palliative for epilepsy, the hope being that just as mistletoe never falls to the ground the same will be true of the patient. The stories live on in some of the Asterix cartoons (which also originated in the land of the Gaul) in which the druid-like character Getafix is shown cutting mistletoe with a sickle before using the plant to brew up a magic potion.

Pieces of mistletoe were once carried by women in many parts of Europe. The mistletoe served as a talisman to ensure fertility. This belief arose from the open-legged nature of female mistletoe twigs festooned with berries that were likened to testicles. The shape of the paired leaves was also compared to that of a woman's ovaries. Mistletoe's reputation for enhancing fertility was incorporated into midwinter festivals along with the excessive consumption of alcohol and a relaxation of the moral code that ensued during the rest of the year. These immoral and more obviously pagan associations with mistletoe resulted in its being banned from most churches until the latter part of the 20th century.

An exception to its exclusion from churches was at York Minster where, until the early 18th century, mistletoe was laid on the altar from Christmas Eve to Twelfth Night as part of a ceremony to pardon 'inferior and wicked people at the gates of the city'. York's heretical acceptance of a pagan symbol and protector against lightning failed to save part of the Minster from a serious fire following a lightning strike in 1984.

PIECES OF MISTLETOE WERE ONCE CARRIED BY WOMEN IN MANY PARTS OF EUROPE. THE MISTLETOE SERVED AS A TALISMAN TO ENSURE FERTILITY.

Despite hostility from the Church, the use of mistletoe as a fertility rite, exemplified by the licence to kiss anyone when standing under it, was very much a part of Old Christmas. This interweaving of pagan and Christian customs held sway in Britain until the Puritans attempted to ban Christmas in the middle of the 17th century. After the restoration of the monarchy (and

Christmas) some of the older customs did not resurface. However, in the 18th century the Revd William Stukeley instigated a revival in the study of the Druids and this led to a renewed interest in mistletoe. He also initiated attempts to introduce it on to more trees, thus improving stocks as the demand for mistletoe at Christmas increased.

At the beginning of the 19th century 'mistletoe kissing' was associated with the working classes, but it became more socially acceptable during the Victorian era when the myth of Balder was resurrected. Even so, it was customary to remove a berry after each kiss and at the loss of all the berries the kissing had to stop. The mistletoe was burnt on Twelfth Night in case any strangers who kissed under it did not intend to marry.

Kissing under the mistletoe is a British custom that has been successfully exported to North America. Several species of mistletoe are found in the States, most with shorter leaves than the British species. The recent innovation of plastic mistletoe has hastened the decline in sales of the real thing. Purists decry the imitation and are further upset by the fact that the shape of the plastic mistletoe is based on an American species.

Despite the decline in sales there is still an active pre-Christmas market supplying mistletoe to wholesalers. In the Worcestershire town of Tenbury Wells there is an auction of mistletoe (together with holly and made-up wreaths) on the last Tuesday in

November and the first two in December. The auction has been a feature of the town for over a hundred years. Much of the mistletoe is supplied by west-country orchard owners and Romany people who all take the opportunity to make some pre-Christmas pin money. Both sellers and buyers were recently upset by a ruling from Brussels making bulk sales of mistletoe liable for VAT.

Since the 19th century, mistletoe has been imported from France and Belgium (where there is no kissing custom) and this has held down the price of the British crop. Apple imports from the same areas have hastened the destruction of English orchards and the removal of fruit trees has destroyed many home-grown sources of mistletoe. The home market received a boost in 1999 when, with the French continuing to ban British beef, there was a backlash against French products. Tesco cancelled a £2 million order for French mistletoe.

A recent survey by Jonathan Briggs has provided an up-to-date snapshot of the current status of mistletoe in Britain. Herefordshire, Worcestershire and Gloucestershire contain the greatest concentrations, closely followed by Somerset. Most other sites are scattered over central, southern and eastern England, with less than 2 per cent of the sightings in the far west (including most of Wales plus Devon and Cornwall) and the north. Mistletoe is very rare in Scotland and Ireland.

The British distribution fits mistletoe's requirements

of a mild, humid climate and sufficient soft-barked trees for the plants to become established, as Richard Mabey points out. The first four counties mentioned earlier have a long history of cultivating apples; 38 per cent of British mistletoe plants grow on cultivated apple trees and some 60 per cent are found in either orchards or gardens. A further 20 per cent of sightings were on common lime, an introduced tree widely planted in parks, churchyards and streets. Hawthorn hedges are another common habitat for mistletoe.

Over 80 per cent of the sightings were on 'human-planted host species'. Mistletoe seed is spread by fruit-eating birds such as the mistle thrush and blackcap, but it is now believed that the majority of our mistletoe plants were deliberately 'sown' to provide plants for Christmas. The most successful sowings were those made some months after Christmas. Mistletoe is very rare on oak. Perhaps it was as a result of this rarity that 'mistletoe oaks' became so important to the Druids. Herefordshire lays claim to seven such trees but nowhere are they common.

Not only is the use of mistletoe on the decline but so too is the plant, at least in its stronghold of Herefordshire, Worcestershire and Somerset. This probably reflects the loss of many old apple orchards in these counties. Happily for future fertility rites the recent survey reported an apparent increase (especially in gardens) in the counties around London.

Holy, Holy, Holly

Holly (*Ilex aquifolium*) is still the plant most widely used for decorating homes and churches at Christmas. Not only is it evergreen, but it fruits throughout the winter when many other plants appear more dead than alive. Like mistletoe, holly plants are either male or female. Add to this the strange spiny leaves and the vivid red berries and it is little wonder that the plant has been steeped in folklore. Long before it became a Christian symbol, holly was an important part of pagan winter festivals throughout Europe.

The Druids believed that the sun never deserted the holly tree even at the winter solstice. The start of the Celtic Samhain was marked by the departure of both the Earth Goddess and the Oak Lord. This left Herne and the Holly Lord to rule over the winter. People decorated their dwellings with branches of holly and other evergreens during the winter in the belief that woodland spirits could find indoor shelter in the greenery during the coldest part of the year. This vegetation was kept inside until Imbolc (early in February) when the Earth Goddess returned and life began to 'spring' anew. After this date it was considered unlucky to have holly (and other evergreens) in the house.

Pliny, the 1st-century Roman writer, recorded that the planting of a holly tree close to a house kept away evil spirits and protected the house from lightning (mistletoe had a similar function). More specifically, Pliny related that holly, like rowan, was thought to provide protection from witches. This belief was associated with the berries as the colour red has long been regarded as having apotropaic (evil-alerting) powers. In medieval times a similar use for holly was as a supposed protection against house goblins. These included one known as Robin Goodfellow. Cutting down a holly tree, rather than just taking off a few small branches, was thought to bring very bad luck.

In many parts of Britain holly was part of the winter fertility rituals. Some holly plants bear strongly prickled leaves and were known as 'he-holly', others have less spiny leaves and were called 'she-holly'. The type of holly brought into the house in late December was said to determine whether the husband or the wife would be the dominant one in the coming year. Overall holly was deemed to represent maleness (despite the custom of collecting berry-bearing branches produced by female trees), in contrast to the supposedly female nature of ivy. Men who carried a holly leaf or berry believed that this made them irresistible to women.

The old Nordic Yule celebrations involved a holly boy and an ivy girl, the two representing male and female as part of ancient fertility rituals. As part of the Roman festival of Saturnalia held in December it was customary to send boughs of evergreens to friends as tokens of good wishes. Though this would have included holly it is likely that holly-like species of evergreen oak, common in areas of southern Europe, were also used.

Holly has fitted well into the Christmas story. Its evergreen habit symbolises the eternal nature of Jesus. The white flowers are a reminder of his immaculate conception and, in a closer reference to the Nativity, of Mary's milk. The berries represent the blood of Christ and prior to the crucifixion holly was said to have had yellow, not red, berries. The leaves were considered a possible source material for the crown of thorns. Holly was also believed to have sprung from the footsteps of Christ and, as with mistletoe, to have provided the wood for making the cross.

The old Church calendar named Christmas Eve as the day for decorating both church and house ('*Templa exornantur*'), it being thought unlucky to do it any earlier. The thick waxy leaves prevented water loss and kept the holly looking fresh for many weeks. The Celts retained holly indoors until Imbolc, early in February, whereas use of evergreens in the Christmas festival is generally for a shorter period. In most parts of Britain it is deemed unlucky if the decorations are not taken down on or by Twelfth Night.

However, older customs prevailed in places where the Christmas greenery was not removed until the eve (day before) of Candlemas. Interestingly, Candlemas is on 2 February, close to Imbolc in the Celtic calendar. The following 17th-century poem by Robert Herrick reminds us of the fusion of pagan and Christmas customs.

Ceremony upon Candlemas Eve

Down with the rosemary, and so
Down with the bays and mistletoe;
Down with the holly, ivy, all
Wherewith ye dress'd the Christmas hall;
That so the superstitious find
No one least branch there left behind;
For look, how many leaves there be
Neglected there, maids, trust to me,
So many goblins you shall see.

Holly was kept even longer in those places where it was used as fuel for cooking the pancakes on Shrove Tuesday. Even when taken down by Twelfth Night many local customs insisted that it be burnt immediately, as recalled in W. H. Auden's poem:

Fading Memory

Well, so that is that. Now we must dismantle
the tree,
Putting the decorations back into their
cardboard boxes –
Some have got broken – and carrying them up
to the attic.
The holly and the mistletoe must be taken
down and burnt,
And the children got ready for school.

Earlier spellings of the name only include one 'l' as in the poem *Grene growth the holy* that dates from the time of Henry VIII. This Christian link is also seen in old alternative names for holly that included Christmas tree, prickly Christmas and Christ's thorn. A good crop of berries was said to predict a long, cold winter (the berries providing necessary food for the birds), but research shows that heavy fruiting is more a result of a previous good season rather than a portent of future bad weather.

In late medieval England holly was used to construct a kissing bough in the form of a loop or crown adorned with coloured paper, fruits, candles and mistletoe. This combined the pagan fertility rites associated with mistletoe, the fire symbol of the candle and the eternal nature of holly. The modern holly wreath, still hung from front doors at Christmas, is a watered-down version of the kissing bough.

As with mistletoe, holly is gathered for the Christmas season and sold on to the wholesale and retail markets. Holly is often collected without the landowner's permission and such poaching can do considerable damage to the trees. Modern mechanical hedge cutters and the grubbing out of many hedges have both affected the availability of holly suitable for the Christmas market. However, Mabey reports that holly is on the increase, especially in upland areas and where there has been a general decline in the number of grazing farm animals that previously kept holly seedlings in check.

Whilst in earlier times evergreens that were part of both pagan and Christian winter customs also included bay (making a comeback through the sale of small potted plants), rosemary and juniper, it is mistletoe, holly and ivy that predominate as the Christmas greenery in 21st-century Britain.

Clingy Ivy and Other Suckers

Oh roses for the flush of youth,
And laurel for the perfect prime;
But pick an ivy branch for me
Grown old before my time.

(Christina G. Rossetti)

Ivy (*Hedera helix*), like holly and mistletoe, is an evergreen perennial. Holly is a tree, mistletoe a semi-parasitic shrub and ivy a woody climber. Ivy clings to walls or trees by means of sucker-like roots, but contrary to popular opinion it is not parasitic on trees, though the added weight of long-established plants may cause tree branches to break. The leathery, glossy leaves vary enormously in both size and shape. Some are hand-like with three or five pointed lobes, but those on flowering stems are more diamond-shaped.

Along with holly and mistletoe, ivy is an evergreen plant bearing winter fruit (clusters of angular, purple-black berries) and has long been believed to have magical powers. Traditionally the plant was dedicated to Bacchus, the god of wine, as it was thought to prevent alcoholic intoxication. Some sources state that this was achieved by the wreath-like binding of the brow, others by drinking the juice from its leaves. An early religious cult of women known as Bacchae became intoxicated with a drink made from ivy and the fly agaric mushroom. At one time it was believed that by filtering wine through small pieces of ivy wood, any water (or more importantly poison) would be held back but it was later discovered that the ivy wood was merely absorbing the colour of the wine. A representation of an ivy plant was formerly displayed over inn doors: the size of the plant on the sign was expected to be proportional to the excellence of the wine supplied.

In Ancient Greece, priests gave a wreath of ivy to newly married couples as an emblem of fidelity. The **MANY OLD CUSTOMS USING IVY TO FORETELL THE FUTURE WERE TRANSFERRED TO THE CHRISTMAS SEASON.** plant has always been looked on as providing good luck for women, and in contrast with the 'male' holly it has long been considered a 'female' plant (the politically incorrect rationale being that it has a clinging nature). This feminine side is clearly indicated in Shakespeare's *A Midsummer Night's Dream* (Act IV, Scene I): 'The female ivy so enrings the barky fingers of the elm.'

Taken together, the 'female' ivy and the 'male' holly were seen as emblems of fertility and good luck. This is alluded to in the well-known carol 'The Holly and the Ivy', though ivy only gets a mention in the first stanza (repeated at the end) and this stanza is possibly part of an older carol added to one about holly. Many old customs using ivy to foretell the future were transferred to the Christmas season. An ivy leaf placed on a dish of water on New Year's Eve was left until Twelfth Night, when a green leaf predicted a healthy year. Brown or black patches forecast problems depending on their position on the leaf (near the apex, problems with legs and feet), while a totally withered leaf was very ominous.

The Christian Church was unhappy about the Bacchanalian associations of ivy. Its use to decorate houses and churches at Christmas was banned by an early Church Council, but its supposed protective power, especially over witches, and its evergreen nature won the day for ivy. Its leaves even feature on medieval carvings in Westminster Abbey.

German, Swedish and Norwegian Wood – The Christmas Tree

While both the holly tree and the hawthorn tree are native angiosperms (flowering plants in which the seeds are protected by the ovary), this is not the case with Norway spruce (*Picea abies*), our traditional Christmas tree. This is not native, having been introduced into Britain some 500 years ago. It is a cone-bearing gymnosperm with naked seeds.

Norway spruce is a fast-growing evergreen, resinous tree with regular whorls of near-horizontal branches. The trunk bark is scaly and the branches decrease in size from the base upwards, resulting in a narrow conical shape. The pointed, dark-green, needle-like leaves are borne singly on wooden projections from the branches. These 'pegs' remain when the 'needles' are shed. Older trees produce clusters of soft, pollen-bearing male 'cones' in early summer and (on the upper branches) solitary dark-red female 'cones'. After fertilisation the latter mature to pendulous, tapering, red-brown cones consisting of overlapping leathery scales that surround the winged seeds.

We have already seen that many pre-Christian customs involved the worship of trees. The decorated maypole at the May Day celebrations and the hanging of loaves from an oak tree at Lammas (loaf mass) – the forerunner of the Christian harvest festival – are just two examples. The notion of a tree of life is one common to many different civilisations.

The direct ancestor of the modern-day Christmas tree appears to have come from the Germanic peoples of central Europe who decorated and worshipped Yule trees in the midwinter season. Several stories have been perpetuated to explain how this pagan custom of worship for a tree became part of the Nativity celebrations and the worship of God.

In the 8th century, the English monk St Boniface was on a missionary visit to Germany when he is said to have introduced worship for the maker of the tree in place of worship of the tree itself. Some versions of the story indicate that he cut down a sacred oak on Christmas Eve and from its roots a fir tree grew. (Fir is a common name for any cone-bearing tree such as spruce and pine.)

A German legend tells of a snowy Christmas Eve when a forester and his family took in a cold, hungry boy who knocked at their door. The family warmed and fed the child before putting him to sleep in their best bed. The following morning, the child, as thanks, broke a branch from a fir tree and planted it by the house door where it immediately blossomed. At this the child predicted that his gift would always bear fruit at Christmas, a dead time of the year, as a sign of undying faith. This story has parallels with that of the Christmas-flowering Glastonbury thorn (see page 236).

Germany was also the setting in medieval times for a play about Adam and Eve in which the Garden of Eden was represented by a fir tree festooned with apples. A so-called Paradise tree, hung with wafers, was later set up in homes on 24 December (Adam and Eve's Day, see page 43). Attempts by the Catholic Church to eradicate tree worship were lifted at the Reformation when, with the spread of the Protestant faith, midwinter tree worship resurfaced in the guise, among other things, of a form of Paradise tree now called the Christmas tree. In the early 16th century, Martin Luther, the leader of the German Reformation, is said to have compared the candles on a decorated

Christmas tree to the starry heavens from which Christ descended at the Nativity.

One of the earliest pictures of a Christmas tree is a 16th-century German painting depicting a man carrying a decorated tree and being blessed by a bishop-like figure on horseback (St Nicholas?). A little later (1605), we get the earliest written record of the German custom: 'At Christmas they set up fir trees in the parlours at Strasburg and hang thereon roses made out of many-coloured paper, apples, wafers, gold-foil, sweets etc.' In other countries, including parts of Austria, only the tip of the fir was decorated and this was hung from the ceiling.

During the 18th and 19th centuries, the Christmas tree custom was spread by German immigrants to many other parts of Europe. It is often recorded that Prince Albert was the first person to introduce the custom to Britain. That he was largely responsible for the rapid spread of the custom is not in doubt, but others were the true innovators. These included a number of German merchants (including a group living in Manchester), German (Hessian) soldiers in the army of George III and German members of the royal court. More significantly Queen Charlotte (wife of George III) included a candle-lit, present-bedecked fir tree as part of her Christmas festivities in the year 1800. Later, in 1821 a member of the court of Queen Caroline (wife of George IV) included a fir branch, decorated with gold-painted fruit, as a decoration for a children's party.

Albert was very keen on the customs of his native

land, and in 1841, a year after his marriage to Queen Victoria, he arranged for a spruce tree to be set up in Windsor Castle. Perhaps what did more to bring this 'new' custom to the attention of the British public was the illustration entitled 'Christmas tree at Windsor Castle' that was published in the Christmas 1848 issue of *Illustrated London News*. This showed the Royal Family gathered round a table on which stood a fir tree adorned with candles and small ornaments. The new custom quickly found its way into literature:

A Christmas Tree

I have been looking on, this evening at a merry company of children assembled round that pretty German toy, a Christmas Tree. The tree was planted in the middle of a great round table, and towered high above their heads. It was brilliantly lighted by a multitude of little tapers; and everywhere sparkled and glittered with bright objects.

(Charles Dickens, writing in *Household Words*)

The Christmas Tree

... on the table in the centre there was placed a great Christmas Tree, hung all over with little lamps and bon-bons, and toys and sweetmeats and bags of cakes. It was the first tree of the kind that I and my companions had ever seen.

It was quite a new fashion the Christmas Tree;
and my brother Tom, who had just come home
from Germany, had superintended its getting
up and decoration.

(Anonymous)

In 1854 a large Christmas tree was placed at the site
of the Great Exhibition, and by 1864 Chamber's *Book of
Days* reported that 'the custom has been introduced
into England with great success'. In the latter half of the
19th century, blown glass baubles were produced as
additions to the tree decorations. In 1882 *Illustrated
London News* included a picture entitled 'Bringing home
the Christmas Tree' and by this time nurseries around
London were growing spruce trees to satisfy the
increasing demand. The previously popular kissing
bough made of evergreens, apples, mistletoe and
candles was gradually replaced by the fir, though for
many years a Christmas tree was restricted to more
wealthy households.

The custom also reached Sweden in the middle of
the 19th century where it too was first adopted by the
upper classes and only became a widespread custom by
the beginning of the 20th century. Since the end of the
Second World War a modern Norse custom has
developed whereby the city of Oslo provides the giant
Norway spruce that is erected in London's Trafalgar
Square in the weeks before Christmas. The tree is a
thank you for Britain's support during the Second

**SHOPPING FOR THE CHRISTMAS TREE IN
COVENT GARDEN**

World War. It is usually about 60 years old and is decorated with over 500 lights.

The Christmas tree also spread to the New World, by way of German mercenaries fighting in the War of Independence and via immigrants from Europe. The custom was certainly spreading in the United States by the 1830s, some years before it caught on in Britain. Trees were sold in New York by the 1850s and in 1891 President Harrison reported that though the plum-pudding was not universal 'the Christmas tree is almost everywhere'. The spruce native to America is sitka spruce (*Picea sitchensis*) and differs not least by having much stiffer needles, making it less forgiving following an accidental brush with its branches. Americans also use balsam and Douglas fir for their trees.

The idea of outside 'communal' trees typified by the one in Trafalgar Square appears to have started in America in 1912 when for the first time a large Christmas tree was put up in New York's Madison Square. Since 1982, the British Christmas Tree Growers' Association has presented a tree to put outside 10 Downing Street. By the end of the 20th century, Christmas trees were common in churches, shops and public buildings. Many people now erect a second tree, festooned with fairy lights, in their front garden.

Fairy lights first appeared in America, around the end of the 19th century. The earliest claim is in 1882 by an employee of the General Electric Company called Edward H. Johnson. He was an associate of Thomas Edison who invented the electric light bulb in 1879. Other sources give the credit to Ralph Morris with a later date of 1895. It was not until the 1920s that the British began to turn their backs on using candles.

Christmas trees have also carried a variety of objects at their apex. During Victorian times this was often a Union Jack flag, but during the 20th century either a star (symbolic of the star in the east) or an angel became more common. The latter reminds us of the story of the visit by the angel of the Lord to inform the shepherds of the birth of Christ. The angel (a messenger of God) on the tree is often mistakenly taken to be a fairy, the problem being partly one of scale.

The traditional Norway spruce, though a convenient shape from which to hang objects or drape lights, is not without its problems – especially that of needle drop in the dry, hot conditions resulting from modern central heating. Ayers, a London firm of industrial cleaners, had the following delightful parody printed on dust bags for vacuum cleaners:

On the Trail of the Lonesome Pine Needle

You'll find them in the budgie's cage
And in the baby's cot.
You can afford to leave no stone
Unturned, no tender foot unsocked.

It's mid-July, you cry out 'Waiter,
What's this in my soup?'
He replies 'Norwegian Tarragon,
According to the cook.'

Partly as a result of the poor needle retention of cut Norway spruce, people have used hairspray to reduce water and hence needle loss, while others go to great lengths to ensure that the cut stump is kept well topped up with water during its seasonal stand. Rooted and container-grown trees have also become more popular, not least as part of a conservation backlash, as they can be replanted. The 'cut' trees mostly end up having to be disposed of and in 2000 this added 9,000 tonnes of waste for disposal.

Artificial trees have been around for about 100 years, with feather trees all the fashion in the 1920s. During the 1970s sales of plastic trees took off. Artificial trees are now much more like real ones and have come down in price in real terms. Despite this, natural trees have made a comeback and are still bought by the vast majority of households where Christmas is celebrated. In 2000, over 6 million natural trees were purchased with a value in excess of £150 million. In the same year Mrs Coulson, living near Swindon, was bitten by an adder that emerged from her natural Christmas tree, where it had been hibernating. She vowed that in future years she would 'buy plastic'.

IN 2000, OVER 6 MILLION NATURAL TREES WERE PURCHASED WITH A VALUE IN EXCESS OF £150 MILLION.

In recent years new cultivars of Norway spruce with better needle retention have been introduced and though this traditional tree remains the cheapest it has been joined by other species of coniferous tree that have different colours, needle shapes (and better retention), aroma and branching patterns. Among the best of these are noble fir, Nordmann fir and blue spruce.

As we move into the 21st century, new fashions include fibre-optic trees. Research (in America) on the genetic engineering of Christmas trees will cut down on insect and fungal attack as well as improving needle retention. Other researchers in the United States have produced cloned Virginia pines that are of a much more regular shape than those grown in the normal way, from seed. High-technology trees are on the way.

Recent work by the Forestry Commission has unearthed the fact that pine needles have been used worldwide as a source of medicine. The needles are high in vitamin C and were once used to treat scurvy. Perhaps more useful at Christmas time is pine needle tea, which has been used for digestive problems and sore heads. Maybe a new hangover cure is waiting in the wings.

All this is a long way from the Norway spruce brought into the Victorian household where it became an important part of the family Christmas. The tree was a place to hang presents from (or under which to hide them), and as a giant candleholder it neatly combined and updated the winter solstice worship of both trees and light. Even the gold and silver baubles may simply represent a more modern form of the gilded apples hung on the original trees in medieval Germany.

Louis Prang and the Evolution of the Christmas Card

Christmas makes the greetings card manufacturers very merry indeed. In the late 1990s the people of Britain purchased some 2,500 million cards annually. Of these nearly 25 per cent were for birthdays, less than 5 per cent for Mother's, Father's and Valentine's Days, but almost 60 per cent of the total were for Christmas. The total annual amount spent on Christmas cards worked out at well over £200 million.

As with many aspects of our modern festival, the Christmas card has its origins in the 18th and 19th centuries. Tradesmen in the 18th century sent New

Year cards to their customers and during this period oral Christmas greetings were reinforced by letters, usually hand-delivered, that accompanied the visiting card of the middle and upper classes. Some authors believe that the Christmas card evolved from Christmas pieces, reward cards or the practice of decorating visiting cards at Christmas, while others look to the Valentine's card that pre-dated its Christmas cousin by about 70 years.

Christmas pieces date from the 18th century and were an early form of feedback from schools to parents as to the progress of their children. The piece was a letter wishing the child's parents the compliments of the Christmas season. It was presented on coloured, often specially produced paper and showed off the child's best 'copperplate' writing. By the start of Victoria's reign such pieces often included quite ornate designs. Reward cards bearing illustrated passages from the scriptures were presented to children for regular Sunday school attendance. After being given reward cards children passed them on to their parents at Christmas when they were displayed on the mantel.

What is generally taken to be the first commercially produced Christmas card dates from 1843, just three years after the introduction of the nationwide penny-post service that had facilitated a cheaper and more reliable way of sending greetings. Prior to the penny-post rate, payment was made on delivery and was based on distance and the number of pieces of paper, so using an envelope incurred more cost. The first card was the idea of Sir Henry Cole, an acquaintance of Prince Albert. He is perhaps better known as the man behind the London Exhibition of 1851 and the first director of the Victoria and Albert Museum.

Cole approached a well-known artist of the day, John Calcott Horsley, whose design was printed lithographically in black and white before each copy was hand-coloured. The central portion of the card showed a family enjoying food and drink, but the fact that the children also seemed to be drinking wine did not go down well with the temperance brigade. The two side panels illustrated examples of charitable acts, those of giving food and clothing. There was no reference to the Nativity. By wishing the recipient 'A Merry Christmas and a Happy New Year To You', it also served as a New Year card. The owner of the shop that sold them stated that many had been sold 'but possibly not more than a thousand'. The cards cost a shilling each, about what a labourer earned in a day and, at twelve times the price of the stamp, this was the equivalent of spending around £2.50 on a card at the end of the 20th century. Given the cost it is not surprising that the first commercially produced Christmas cards were not a great success.

Several developments over the following 30 years were to change the fortunes of Christmas card manufacturers. The first, less than a year after Cole's card, was the invention of an envelope-making machine. More importantly, cheaper forms of colour printing, including chromolithography, considerably reduced production costs. Finally the introduction in 1870 of a special halfpenny postage rate for cards in unsealed envelopes was a major contributor to the increasing popularity (among the upper and middle classes at least) of sending Christmas cards. A letter to *The Times* in 1877 complained of the delay to legitimate correspondence by cartloads of children's cards and 1880 saw the first plea to 'post early for Christmas'. By the end of the 1880s cheap cards cost closer to a penny than a shilling and annual card sales had topped a million.

A similar development took place in America where the work of Louis Prang, a Bavarian-born lithographer who had emigrated to Boston, led the way. Prang helped to advertise his new printing technique by way of a card bearing a Christmas message, and by the early 1880s he was producing over 5 million cards every year. By the 1890s some cards cost as little as one cent, others as much as one dollar.

Early cards were small and not folded. By the 1880s larger, folded cards became more popular. The designs of the cards were many and varied. Some publishers employed top artists of the day (such as Kate Greenaway) and others ran competitions for new designs.

In the 1880s *The Times* started an annual review of Christmas cards and this was later taken up by other national papers. In 1883 *The Illustrated London News* published its first Christmas card survey which showed that out of 27 categories of design, only two were religious in nature. Scenes of country houses in the snow and skaters on frozen ponds were the most common, as was the snow-bound mail coach. The latter was a nostalgic reference to 1836 when deep snow crippled the pre-penny-post service.

Greenery (especially holly and mistletoe) soon became an integral part of the designs and so too did the Christmas pudding and other mainstays of Christmas food. Designs included animals, children, hunting scenes and flowers, with the poinsettia an early example of the latter. Many card designs were very similar to those already in use for Valentine cards. Others included the image of a ship, some with the Christ child at the helm. The picture of a ship coming in to port ('my ship is coming in') has long been a symbol of prosperity and luck. Father Christmas featured from the 1870s in a variety of different-coloured garments.

Many of the top Victorian artists and designers were employed in what became an increasingly competitive business. Humour was also much in evidence, though some of the comic cards were rather bizarre and vulgar. As elsewhere in Victorian society the thin veneer of respectability was stripped away by Christmas cards depicting naked young girls. A more respectable bird was the robin; these appeared on cards as early as the 1850s and soon became a firm favourite. The story behind this link is told on page 181.

It was not long before cards were being augmented with material or frosting and there were even squeaking cards (the forerunner of the modern singing card). Edwardian cards were influenced by art nouveau together with recent inventions such as cars and aeroplanes. The picture postcard also had an effect on the design of Edwardian cards. The coming of the First World War saw a drop in the number of cards sent but many military regiments produced their own cards for mailing *from* the front. Greetings carried by cards going *to* the front are exemplified by one sent from 'The Princess Mary and Friends at Home', which included this message:

> With Best Wishes
> for a Happy Christmas
> and a Victorious New Year.

Between the wars art deco was an important influence. Cards bearing the reproduction of a famous painting became big sellers. Though sales dipped again in the Second World War, they have continued to rise over the past 50 years. In the 1950s the weather was an important theme, with snowy scenes predominating along with lots of people dressed in Victorian costume. Glitter was common but Father Christmas was scarce. Through the 1960s and 1970s colours intensified, paper quality improved and new designs such as those initiated by the Gordon Fraser company began to replace some of the Victorian scenes. Artistic licence was held to account in the mid 1980s by Colin Fairclough, who wrote to the *Daily Telegraph*:

Every year we are confronted with scenes of the Nativity events at Bethlehem in which the chief architectural features are mosques and minarets. Picturesque, no doubt, but several centuries ahead of their time.

Now, 160 years on from the first commercially produced Christmas card, many of the themes are the same, though cats and dogs have been joined by Christmas teddy bears. Old masters are still with us, especially those showing the Madonna, the Magi or the shepherds. Although the first did not appear until the 1940s it was not until the latter part of the 20th century that the charity card came into its own, with over £100 million spent on such cards in the year 2000. Even here the design is important and can override the buyer's desire to support a certain charity. Green concerns have resulted in an increased number of cards being printed on recycled card or on material from 'managed forests'. Despite e-mail and text messages, the number of Christmas cards sent has increased each year since the final decade of the 20th century.

DESPITE E-MAIL AND TEXT MESSAGES, THE NUMBER OF CHRISTMAS CARDS SENT HAS INCREASED EACH YEAR.

Humorous cards account for less than 10 per cent of the market, though even here traditional themes abound. A 1990s card asked 'How do you stop a robin feeling hungry at Christmas?' and gave the answer 'Hit it with a shovel'. Another form of robin has surfaced as an American import: the middle-class round-robin letter that is slipped in with the card (or e-mailed with a full-colour attachment in lieu of a card). This takes the form of a review of the family year and is full of accounts of wonderful holidays and impressive exam or sporting achievements by the children, frequently tempered by gory details of family illnesses and pet deaths.

Recently, psychologists have analysed the Christmas card market. Professor Adrian Furnham provides us with insights such as 'A handmade card suggests a creative person who has time on his hands'. Wealth and status go with cards that include a printed personal message but 'the Skodas of the card world are those that play a jolly tune when you open them'.

No doubt the 21st century will bring new fashions as the Christmas card continues to evolve. Lest we forget the origins of the custom, it is worth noting that just before the 2001 Christmas season an original Horsley card of 1843 (only 12 are still known to exist) came up for auction in Devizes. The card was sold for £20,000. Perhaps we should think twice before discarding our old ones.

Rasta Colours, Lame Jokes and Love Poems – The Christmas Cracker

Whether perched on the horizontal branches of a Christmas tree (which started to become popular in Britain only a few years before the cracker was introduced) or as part of the place settings for the Christmas meal, crackers have become an integral part of many Christmas celebrations. Crackers also find a place at birthday parties and other occasions, but their first appearance was as part of the Victorian Christmas.

The year 1997 was fêted as the 150th anniversary of the invention of the cracker and our Christmas stamps of that year featured Father Christmas and crackers. The first-class stamp pictured a cracker on which there was a picture of a child wearing a hat. Most crackers include a paper hat, and this encouragement to wear a party hat is an interesting throwback to the Roman Saturnalia celebrations when the participants also wore hats.

The idea for the cracker goes back to slightly earlier than 1847, which is when a Mr Tom Smith set up his firm in Finsbury Square, London. Mr Smith had started work as a boy in an ornamental confectioner's shop in London making pralines, fondants and pastilles before setting up his own business making wedding cake decorations and selling

THE IDEA OF THE CRACK MECHANISM IS SAID TO HAVE BEEN PROMPTED BY THE CRACKLE OF A LOG BURNING IN HIS FIREPLACE.

sweets. It was during a visit to Paris that he came across the bon-bon, a sugared almond wrapped in tissue paper (with a twist either side of the centrally placed sweet) and decided to try selling similarly wrapped sweets in the lead-up to Christmas. Among these was the sugared almond that had been popular in England since the Tudor period.

His bon-bons sold well at Christmas, in an era when sweets were not generally wrapped, but sales fell away after Christmas. In the early 1850s Tom Smith came up with the idea of including a motto with the sweet. As most of his bon-bons were bought by men to give to women, many of the mottoes were simple love poems such as:

Sunshine, happiness and laughter
Be yours now and ever after

The sweet crimson rose with its beautiful hue
Is not half so deep as my passion for you.

The third element of Smith's wrapped sweet was the addition (in about 1860) of two pieces of chemically impregnated paper that made a loud noise on being pulled apart. The idea of the crack mechanism is said to have been prompted by the crackle of a log burning in his fireplace. At first these novelties were called 'cosaques', but they soon became known by the more English-sounding name of 'crackers'. For some the bangs are a reminder of the revelry and noise associated with the celebration of Christmas in former times.

Unfortunately for Mr Smith other manufacturers copied his idea, so to stay ahead of the competition he made yet another change – this time he discarded the sweet and replaced it with a surprise gift. The type and cost of the gift enabled him to make a great range of crackers to suit different markets.

When Tom Smith died (and there is still a memorial fountain to his wife Martha close to the original factory site in east London), his two sons Tom and Walter continued with the business. It was Tom junior who came up with the final addition, that of a paper hat, and these were becoming common in crackers by the early Edwardian period. By the end of the 1930s the love poems had been replaced by limericks or jokes that gradually evolved into the puns and *double entendres* found in the modern cracker, such as:

Question: What's musical and handy in a supermarket?
Answer: A Chopin Liszt!

The quality and theme of the novelty gift has included streamers, tape measures, whistles and conjuring tricks. Today these are often made of plastic in the cheaper versions but, as more firms began manufacturing crackers, some boxes such as those made by the Crown Jewellers, Asprey and Garrard, sold for up to £5000 with crackers bearing gold trinkets nestling in suede pouches. Despite this competition Tom Smith's firm dominated the market for a century, a position much helped in 1906 when the Prince of Wales featured Smith crackers at one of his parties. The firm has held many royal warrants, including one for the Queen since 1964. It has also produced crackers for important occasions such as the Paris Exhibition in 1900.

In 1927 a man sent a diamond engagement ring to

Tom Smith's firm asking that it be placed in a cracker and sent to a young lady. He enclosed ten shillings to pay for the cracker and delivery but unfortunately forgot to enclose an address for either the lady or himself. The ring, letter and ten-bob note were kept for many years in the company safe. In 1998 the firm (now based near Norwich) was bought by Napier Industries, who continue to supply the Royal Family. Their annual sales top 45 million boxes. Although crackers have been produced in many different colours, the highest sales are for those that are coloured red, green or gold.

Candles, Wartime Shortages and Groundhog Day

As the eldest child in a large family my mother had a special job at Christmas during the 1920s. When the candles on the Christmas tree were lit she had to stand near the tree with a jug of water in case any of the foliage caught alight. Martin Luther's 16th-century comparison of a candle-lit tree with the starry heaven from which Christ descended has been slightly dimmed by the substitution of fairy lights for candles, but elsewhere candles are still much in evidence as part of the modern Christmas.

The burning of lamps and candles to lighten the dark days of the European midwinter pre-dated Christianity by thousands of years. They were lit as part of a process to keep evil spirits at bay and renew the power of the sun (and with it promote fertility) around the time of the shortest day. Lighting candles is another example of the burning tree ceremony, as is the Yule log tradition.

To many early Christians, candles and other lights were much in evidence during December as part of the Roman Saturnalia celebrations. They also feature in the Jewish Hanukkah or festival of lights, commemorating the rededication of the Temple in 165 BC after Judas Maccabees had triumphed over the Syrian tyrant Antiochus. During the festival, candles are burnt on a candelabrum of seven or nine branches known as a Menorah or Hanukkiya. A derivation of this in the form of seven candle-like bulbs on a stepped base has recently become popular as a Christmas windowsill decoration.

IN VICTORIAN TIMES GROCERS PRESENTED THEIR VALUED CUSTOMERS WITH A LARGE YULE CANDLE AT CHRISTMAS.

In Victorian times grocers presented their valued customers with a large Yule candle at Christmas. Before the introduction of the Christmas tree, candles were to be found as part of the Advent wreath and kissing bough, incorporating sprays of holly, ivy and other evergreens. On the first Sunday in Advent one of the candles was lit, on the second two, until the fourth Sunday when all four were lit. This custom is now much less common in Britain and has largely been replaced by a single candle that is burnt for a short time on each day in Advent. Some Advent wreaths included a fifth candle (the Christ candle) to be burnt on either

Christmas Eve or Christmas Day in commemoration of Christ's birth.

The best candles were made from beeswax. This has the advantage that, when purified and bleached, it provides a largely odourless fuel to keep the wick burning. However, it has only ever been available in a limited supply, so candles made from beeswax are expensive. The traditional alternative came from tallow, produced by rendering animal fats. This was cheap but its main disadvantage was its unsavoury smell. Palm oil is another source material, but paraffin wax, a by-product of the petroleum industry, is now the most widely used candle fuel.

Just as one company (Tom Smith's) was for many years the main producer of crackers in Britain, so another business dating from the 19th century has long been associated with the manufacture of candles. The firm of Price's was started in 1830 by Benjamin Lancaster and William Wilson. They named it after their maiden aunt, Miss E. Price. At that time everyone used candles, and the company, based in Thames-side London near Battersea, flourished and grew to employ nearly 2,000 people.

Price's also made soap and was eventually sold to Lever Brothers (detergent makers) in 1922. During the 1930s paraffin wax became more widely available and since then it has provided the raw material for cheaper candles made at the factory. Candles were in short supply during the Second World War when blockades reduced the import of oil and its products. The firm was later bought by a group of oil companies. By the latter half of the 20th century there had been a considerable downturn in the candle business, not least as a result of a reliable supply of electricity for lighting. By the 1990s cheap imported candles from China and other parts of the Far East further hit Price's (and prices).

When in danger of closure the firm was bought in 1991 by a former financier, Richard Simpson. Since then candle sales have increased by over 50 per cent as a result of a renaissance in demand for candles, whether as part of an intimate meal, an outdoor barbecue or an aromatherapy session (often used to de-stress people who have been 'burning the candle at both ends'). An estimated billion candles were burnt in Britain in the year 2000. Christmas remains the most important time for sales (especially of red candles) as we burn more candles on Christmas Day than on any other day of the year. Unfortunately, the revival of candle power has been accompanied by an increased number of house fires, the result of untended candles (19 deaths in 1999) – a salutary reminder to give smoke alarms as Christmas presents.

As a protection against winter demons, the Celtic Druids and other European pagan groups kept house fires and lights burning through the midwinter period until early in February. On that date, known as Imbolc, they believed that the Earth goddess returned from her midwinter visit to the other world. The medieval Christian church incorporated part of this tradition by burning candles through the Twelve Nights of Christmas.

In the church calendar, 2 February marks the purification of Mary after the birth of Christ. Part of the festival involved the lighting of candles and the day became known as Candlemas. Some church services on 2 February still include a candle-bearing procession. This day, 2 February, is also Groundhog Day, a modern American custom borrowed from Europe, where it began as an ancient pagan custom. The antics of an animal waking from hibernation (and the presence or lack of its shadow) are said to indicate whether the worst of the winter is over.

In the 20th century, Britain imported a candle custom from America that originated in 1747 with the Moravian Church in Germany. The celebration of Christingle, a word meaning 'Christ-light', has been endorsed by, among others, the Children's Society. Special church services are held close to Christmas (traditionally on Christmas Eve) in which children from the congregation receive, and often process with, a Christingle. This consists of four cocktail sticks carrying nuts, sweets and dried fruits set in an orange encompassed by a red ribbon. On top of the orange is a candle. The orange represents the (God-created) world, the sticks the four seasons, the food God's gifts and the lighted candle Jesus, the Light of the World. The red ribbon represents the blood of Christ.

Pagans, Chaucer and the Rebel 18th-century Carollers

Carols epitomise Christmas, but for many hundreds of years they were not a part of church services throughout much of Britain. As explained on page 227, the churches and chapels of Wales have long had their own special carol service at Christmas, but at the time of the Christmas books by Dickens (mid-19th century) church-based carol services were almost unknown in England and Scotland. From the mid-17th century carols were sung at home, in the street and at other gatherings, but only rarely within the established church. They were formally re-instigated by the Church of England in 1878 at a service held at 10pm on Christmas Eve in Truro. Since then church carol services have become firmly embedded in the Christmas calendar.

Although the modern definition of a carol is a Christmas hymn, the older meaning was of a joyful song and the word probably comes from the French *carole* meaning a ring-dance with a song. In their earliest form carols were more a mix of pagan dances and chants, often in the form of a ring or circle dance, performed outdoors. Interestingly, two early names for Stonehenge were Giants' Dance and Giants' Carol. These pagan winter carols were typically associated with fertility rites and the winter solstice. It was these pagan links and the lack of an association with Christmas (only its season) that resulted in carols being banned from churches.

Religious connections with carols began to appear around the 12th century, from when they became a part of different festivals such as Easter, in addition to Christmas. It is noticeable that even those medieval carols specifically about Christmas such as 'Boar's Head Carol', made little if any mention of the Nativity and concentrated instead on the pleasures of food and drink associated with Christmas.

In the 14th century Chaucer wrote:

'Come, and if it lyke you
To dauncen dauncith with us now.'
And I, without tarrying,
Wente into the karolying.

By this time the Church's resistance to carols had subsided (though carols were still condemned by some Church Councils as late as 1435) and the period from 1400 to 1647 saw many new ones written. This era came to an end after the Reformation with the rise of the Puritans who abhorred all pagan links with Christmas and outlawed the public singing of Christmas carols. The restoration of Charles II did little to restore the place of the Christmas carol. Carols continued to be cold-shouldered by the Church of England and for the following two centuries they were hardly heard in church or in the houses of the well-off. Only dissenters and radicals kept the carol tradition alive throughout the 18th century.

For much of the 18th century the only carol

permitted in services of the Anglican Church was 'While Shepherds Watched Their Flocks by Night'. This was based on Luke's Gospel account and written in the late 17th century by Tate and Brady, two members of the Church of Ireland. Despite the antagonism

ONLY DISSENTERS AND RADICALS KEPT THE CAROL TRADITION ALIVE THROUGHOUT THE 18TH CENTURY.

of the Anglican Church, several well-known carols were written in the 18th century, including 'O Come All Ye Faithful' and 'Christians Awake'. Charles Wesley's 'Hark the Herald Angels Sing' even found its way into Anglican services by the end of the 18th century.

Shortly before Victoria came to the throne carols began to regain their popularity and many local, almost forgotten carols were collected and published. Carols once again became accepted by all classes as part of the nostalgia for the Christmas of 'Merrie Olde England'. Among the carols that were written during the Victorian period are 'Good King Wenceslas' and 'Good Christian Men, Rejoice'. Settlers in some parts of North America never lost their passion for carols and some well-known 19th-century carols, often believed to be of British origin, were actually written in America. These include 'Away in a Manger', 'We Three Kings' and 'O Little Town of Bethlehem'.

Away from churches, carols have traditionally been sung outside houses in the evenings leading up to Christmas Day. The custom, known as 'the waits', may have evolved from the watchmen of the 18th century who announced (often with music) the watches (times)

of the night. Their 'carolling' was later taken up by church choirs and small groups of children, the latter frequently with little religious or musical sense, but keen to share the bounty from the collecting tin. Such traditions continued in successive centuries and Laurie Lee, in *Cider with Rosie*, recounts one such evening of 'carol-barking':

> We were the Church Choir, so no answer was necessary. For a year we had praised the Lord out of key, and as a reward for this service – on top of the Outing – we now had the right to visit all the big houses, to sing our carols and collect our tribute.
>
> As we went down the lane other boys, from other villages, were already about the hills, bawling 'Kingwenslush', and shouting through keyholes 'Knock on the knocker! Ring at the bell! Give us a penny for singing so well!' They weren't an approved charity as we were, the Choir; but competition was in the air.

In parts of Somerset, Cornwall, Derbyshire and South Yorkshire there is a tradition dating back to the 19th century of singing carols in pubs. In two villages just outside Sheffield (Dungworth and Worrall) pub regulars, each with their own repertoire (including local carols that originated in non-conformist chapels), attract people from far and wide on the Sundays leading up to Christmas. Many of the carols' titles reflect local place names and the singing of these village carols is loud and vigorous. Some of the current performers represent their family's fourth generation of singers. Most are there for the beer and the joy of singing 'Christmas folk songs' in a manner closer to the old meaning of the word carol.

The 1878 church carol service in Truro consisted of a sermon, prayers and two lessons interspersed with carols. Two years later it became nine lessons and carols, and when the then Bishop of Truro, Edward Benson, became Archbishop of Canterbury the festival of nine lessons (some from the Old and some from the New Testament) and carols went with him. In 1918 the Dean of King's College Cambridge took up the theme in an afternoon service on Christmas Eve. Since it was first broadcast in 1930, this service has become, for many, the start of Christmas.

The service always starts with a treble soloist singing the first verse of 'Once in Royal David's City', but the other carols are typically a mix of well-known and lesser-known titles. Among the former may be 'Silent Night', a carol that has attracted its own folklore. A day before Christmas 1818 mice are said to have incapacitated the church organ in Oberndorf, just outside Salzburg. The Christmas Eve service was saved by the first performance of a hurried composition of 'Silent Night' set for vocals and guitar. The words are accredited to a local priest, one Joseph Mohr, and the music to Franz Gruber, church organist and music teacher.

It is now evident that the words, at least, were written two years before the 1818 Christmas, which casts doubt on the mouse story. The peace normally equated with 'Silent Night' has been further upset by the contention that Gruber was merely responsible for arranging the music that, along with the words, may have been written by Mohr. This has not gone down well in Salzburg and its museum honouring the highly respected Gruber, especially as Mohr was the bastard son of an army deserter and a frequenter of taverns. War has been declared between the Gruber and Mohr supporters. As detailed on page 68, 'Silent Night' also played its part in the Great War, almost 100 years after it was written.

Carols have thrown up a few anomalies. King Wenceslas would hardly have been remembered but for the carol. History shows him to have been a 10th-century ruler of Bohemia, originally an independent kingdom that changed hands many times and was, until 1949, a province of Czechoslovakia. Wenceslas was apparently a good ruler but was murdered by his less scrupulous brother in the year 929. Carols have also extrapolated the bleak midwinter image to the events of the Nativity, which probably took place during a Middle Eastern summer. As *The Times* leader for 21 December 2001 commented: 'Snow does not fall, snow on snow, even in the deepest midwinter at Bethlehem.' The desire for a white Christmas is deeply entrenched ...

The Tame, Tyrannical Robin Redbreast

The robin (*Erithacus rubecula*) is Britain's best-known and best-loved bird, so much so that it is often labelled Britain's national bird. It is found throughout the British Isles as a resident species and breeds across the country with the exception of Shetland and some other islands off the north of Scotland. Common in gardens, it is also frequent in town parks and churchyards in addition to hedgerows and its original woodland habitat.

Its close association with humans has helped it become well known, but it is its tameness, especially during severe winter weather (when food is in short supply), that has endeared it to the British. This relationship with people can be traced back to our medieval coppiced woodlands. Woodcutters, charcoal burners and other craftspeople were regular visitors to these woods and some even lived where they worked. Originally a bird of our native wild wood, the robin quickly adapted to live in more managed woodland from where it spread to hedges, parks and gardens.

The tameness of British robins is not shared by those that are resident on mainland Europe where it is typically a shy, retiring bird. This is partly a result of the widespread shooting of small birds that has long been practised on the continent. Not only do British robins enter kitchens in search of food, they also take a close interest in garden cultivation, keeping an eye out for worms. Robins are also famous for their catholic tastes in nesting sites that include old cars, boots and watering cans. Normally some five or six eggs are laid and incubated by the female for about a fortnight.

Robins have long been considered omens of good luck (or the reverse if killed or caged) and in many parts of Britain it was the custom to make a wish on seeing the first robin of the year. This supposed luck-bringing quality is probably linked to its red breast. Red is often thought of as the colour to ward off evil, especially from witches (hence the use of red-berried holly and rowan). The second part of the bird's Latin name, *rubecula*, alludes to this red colour (as in ruby). Some other British birds, such as redstart and redwing, also have a chestnut-red breast, but the robin is the only one with such a bright red colour that also covers its face. Unusually both male and female adult robins sport the red breast; in most other species of bird the colourful plumage is restricted to the male.

ROBINS HAVE LONG BEEN CONSIDERED OMENS OF GOOD LUCK (OR THE REVERSE IF KILLED OR CAGED) AND IN MANY PARTS OF BRITAIN IT WAS THE CUSTOM TO MAKE A WISH ON SEEING THE FIRST ROBIN OF THE YEAR.

The small size of the robin (about 14 cm or 5½ inches from bill tip to end of tail) contributes to its cuteness. The sweet warbling song of a robin continues even amid the frost and snow of midwinter. The singing helps to protect a robin's territory. Robins are very territorial and, despite the cuddly image, males can be very aggressive towards one another.

In addition to its reputation as a bird of good luck there are many other myths about the robin. Robins have been given almost human traits in stories where their tenderness to the suffering and the dead is portrayed. In an original version of the Babes in the Wood story it was a robin that covered the sleeping children with leaves. This same caring trait is also part of a number of religious robin stories. Many of these are fanciful explanations of how the bird got its red breast. One story involves a robin visiting souls burning in hell and taking them water to ease their suffering. During this merciful act its breast was scorched by fire. A more well-known legend is that of a robin trying to relieve Christ's suffering on the cross by removing part of his crown of thorns. In doing so the robin's breast became covered with the blood of Jesus and this red colour has remained. Some authors quote this story as being behind the robin/Christmas link, but I consider this to be an Easter story.

There is another story, however, that comes closer to providing an allegorical link between the Nativity and robins:

The night after Jesus was born was a very cold one and the fire that Joseph had made to keep Mary and the infant Christ warm had burnt low. Joseph was away in search of more wood and

Mary was concerned that the fire would go out before his return. At this point a number of small brown birds flew in to the stable and having made a circle round the dying fire they started to fan it with their wings. This rejuvenated the fire and kept it alight until Joseph returned with more fuel.

So Mary and the Babe were kept warm but Mary noticed that in their efforts to fan the fire they had scorched their breasts and she said to them, 'Because of the love you have shown my child, in future you little brown birds will have fiery red breasts in memory of the good that you have done. People will love you and call you Robin Redbreast.'

This rather implausible story has never been well-known enough to explain the popularity of the robin as a symbol of Christmas. It is undoubtedly due in part to the robin's boldness during cold winter weather. Like holly and ivy, the bird is most noticeable in the Christmas season. There is also a more spurious link, this time with Father Christmas. In earlier times the present-bringer was often aided by a 'dark helper'. In post-Shakespearean Britain this dark helper was frequently depicted as the Pan figure known as Robin Goodfellow. Cards showing a robin perched on Father Christmas may be the last remnants of an older version of the Father Christmas story.

There is, however, a more easily acceptable

explanation as to why robins feature on so many Christmas cards. The link was first brought to my attention by the detective work of David Lack, one of the pioneers of ornithological research and author of *The Life of the Robin*. Lack pointed out that the custom of sending Christmas cards started only a few years after the introduction of the universal penny-post service in Britain. For at least two decades, postmen wore red coats and this resulted in their being given the nickname of 'robin'. Lack concluded that initially the bird represented not Christmas but the bringer of Christmas tidings, the postman himself. As early as 1869 a cartoon in *Punch* was headed 'I wish someone would invent a new felicitation card. I hate those Redbreasts'.

Robins are usually depicted on Christmas cards as part of a snowy scene. As it happens, robins, like other small birds, are very vulnerable to bad winters. This is graphically illustrated by the British Trust for Ornithology's census returns, which show a marked fall in robin numbers after the bad winter of 1962/63 followed by a build-up through the rest of the 1960s and 1970s until the very snowy winter of 1978/79. Recent wet, less cold winters have favoured the Christmas robin.

It is not only *Punch* that has refused to fall for the robin's cute image. This is clearly seen in a letter to David Lack by another research ornithologist, Richard Meinertzhagen:

[The robin] is certainly the last to bed and the earliest up which fits with his greed and aggression. He has all the characteristics of Mussolini and I know of no bird less suited to association with the birth of the Messiah.

Gold, Frankincense, Myrrh and other Christmas Presents

6 January, also known as Twelfth Day (the twelfth day *after* Christmas, see page 48), is the feast of Epiphany in the Western Christian Church. The Epiphany story is that of the manifestation of Christ to the Gentiles (non-Jewish peoples) in the form of the Magi (Wise Men). During the 19th century and for all but the last year of Victoria's reign, 6 January was also Christmas Day under the old calendar. It is thus perhaps not surprising that the present-giving custom, though commemorating the presents brought by the Magi, has become linked not to 6 January but 25 December.

In fact, as with so many Christmas customs, the giving of presents was borrowed from pre-Christian winter festivals, especially the Roman feast of Saturnalia and the New Year Kalends celebration. As part of the week-long Saturnalia celebration the rich gave gifts to the poor (who responded with garlands), while money gifts at New Year were said to ensure prosperity (possibly the origin of the Scottish New

Year custom when 'first footers' enter a house bearing coal and salt).

In Britain it was not until the 1860s that present giving became more associated with Christmas Day than the New Year, a change partly encouraged by the arrival of Moore's poem from America. At that time it was not customary to wrap presents (the element of surprise, for the children at least, came from the fact that the presents were kept in a locked room prior to Christmas Eve). Today the green movement bemoans the waste associated with present giving: 270,000 tonnes of packaging from Christmas presents in the year 2000, including 83 square kilometres of wrapping paper.

What do we know of the original Christmas gifts of gold, frankincense and myrrh as presented by the Magi? Much has been made of the symbolic nature of these three gifts, with gold representing the wealth fit for a king, frankincense standing for divinity and spirituality, and myrrh reflecting the suffering that Jesus endured on the cross. The practical value of gold is obvious, but what of frankincense and myrrh?

Both frankincense and myrrh come from a family of plants known as the Burseraceae, in which all parts of the plants, especially the bark, contain a resin. It is the dried resin of both species that is traded, as it has been for thousands of years. Frankincense comes from *Boswellia carteri*, a small tree native to Somalia on the horn of East Africa, while myrrh is from *Commiphora abyssinica* and the related *C. molmol*, both of which are spiny shrubs found in Ethiopia and Arabia. Incisions made in the bark release the liquid resin that hardens into reddish brown, teardrop-shaped lumps. Both resins are highly aromatic and have long been used as constituents of incense, the burning of which produces strong, sweet-smelling fumes.

Frankincense was mainly used to cover smells, the burning of the resin releasing a powerful fragrance. Myrrh was more valuable, especially as a medicine. The resins and associated essential oils have antiseptic and possibly antibiotic properties – useful after a birth in a room also used by animals. Both resins were used (often in association with honey) for dressing wounds, where the ability of frankincense to stem bloodflow was equally as important. They also served as mouthwashes for gum and tooth infections and to alleviate catarrh. Both resins were much used in Ancient Egypt as part of the mummification process. The Egyptian Queen Hatshepsut sent an expedition to Somalia nearly 3,500 years ago to collect *Boswellia* plants. The trees were established at Karnak and a record of this was carved on the temple walls.

Myrrh was thought to have pain-relieving properties and was a constituent (along with wine/vinegar, hyssop and mandrake) in the soporific sponge offered to the victims of crucifixion. Jesus is said to have refused this palliative, but his body was anointed with myrrh on being taken down from the cross.

Frankincense and myrrh do not grow outdoors in Britain, but one plant that does is an aniseed-scented relative of cow parsley known as sweet cicely. Because of its aroma it is sometimes called myrrh and this is reflected in its Latin name, *Myrrhis odorata*. It has long been used as a sweetener during the cooking of rhubarb and sour apples. The plant flowers very early in the year and in the Isle of Man it was believed to flower as early as Christmas Eve (as with the Glastonbury thorn on page 236), before the changeover to the Gregorian calendar.

At an Epiphany service held in the Chapel Royal at St James's Palace in London, the monarch's representative presents symbolic offerings of gold, frankincense and myrrh. Money, to the value of 25 gold sovereigns, is distributed to the needy, frankincense goes for church use and myrrh is sent to a local hospital. The supposed remains of the Magi were taken from Constantinople (now Istanbul) to Milan and finally in 1164 to a shrine in Cologne Cathedral to which many people still make a pilgrimage. Epiphany is also the day when the Pope traditionally ordains new bishops.

Today, present giving is an important part of Christmas. For young children it is wrapped up with the story of Santa Claus and for the retail trade it accounts for a massive increase in spending. Fashions have changed through the years, though some items remain popular. In the 1880s dolls became the sought-after present after some were purchased by Queen Victoria for her children. By 1900 elegant black corsets were the 'in' gift for ladies, and fancy (some would say impractical) lingerie has remained on many Christmas shopping lists since then. In 2001 Merry Christmas thongs, tastefully hidden inside Christmas crackers, were a modern example of this theme.

In the mid-1930s, hats, gloves and scarves were important accessories for those spending time in the unheated motor car of the day. The Second World War not only brought a significant reduction in the amount spent on presents but also the introduction of unusual gift items such as a combined gas mask carrier and handbag. Gloves, scarves and slippers are still popular (with senders if not recipients) and in 1999 gifts of clothing and footwear totalled nearly £3.5 billion, nearly as much as that spent on toys and other gifts.

By the 1960s toys were the most important sector of the Christmas present market, with each year since then being dominated by a 'must-have' present. Lego filled this spot in 1960, 20 years later it was Rubik's cube and in 1990 Teenage Mutant Hero Turtles were all the rage. Over one Christmas the Thunderbirds' Tracy Island was more like gold in rarity value. Barbie and Action Man have both outlasted more transient crazes and it remains to be seen how long Harry Potter will survive near the top spot. The days when children were pleased to find some gloves and an orange in their stocking have long gone.

For adults, expensive perfumes have long been a favourite Christmas present, a theme rather closer to

BY THE 1960S TOYS WERE THE MOST IMPORTANT SECTOR OF THE CHRISTMAS PRESENT MARKET, WITH EACH YEAR SINCE THEN BEING DOMINATED BY A 'MUST-HAVE' PRESENT.

the original gifts of frankincense and myrrh. As a twenty-year-old, sporting my two-year-old beard, I received as a Christmas present the inevitable after-shave from a distant, rarely seen, uncle – this required a few white lies in the thank-you letter. In 1999 over £1.5 billion was spent on electrical goods for Christmas, with computers and computer games replacing many of the more traditional gifts. As for Christmas 2000, it was the year of the mobile phone. With the average retailer seeing 20 per cent of their annual sales in the single month of December, Christmas is very important to the modern economy.

Many family pets first arrive as Christmas presents, though sadly not all are appreciated as the festive season ends, hence the significance of the slogan 'A dog is for life, not just for Christmas'. For the happy pet owner there is now a full range of presents for pets and these include special crackers and even pet chocolate. We will have to await future fashions in present giving, but hopefully one American custom will never be allowed in Britain – in 2001 some 200,000 guns were presented as Christmas gifts in the United States, half of them youth-sized.

For many children the excitement of receiving presents is somewhat muted by the chore of having to write thank-you letters. Computers have made this much easier and enabled children to write a common letter and then customise each one with the details of the present. Older readers may remember an amusing manual version of this wheeze as executed by

Molesworth. A phoned thank you is rather more common today and in the future the text message may become the norm as a way of saying thank you.

Boxing Day was traditionally the day when gifts were given to tradesmen and some households still give a seasonal present to, among others, their postman. These days such an offering needs to be made before the Christmas shutdown.

Pantomime-an Excuse for Cross-dressing Since Ancient Times

As with so much of the entertainment that is a part of the modern Christmas festivities, the origins of pantomime are to be found in a strange mixture of former theatrical events. Two thousand years ago the Roman people were entertained by their version of pantomime (the Latin *mimus* means mime), where the masked principal actor mimed and danced a variety of roles while a chorus supplied the storyline. The characters portrayed were satirised and ridiculed in a burlesque style that included nakedness and lewd scenes. In the 5th century, following the rise of Christianity, many actors were excommunicated and later theatres were closed down.

Ironically, some of the elements of pantomime survived in the great religious festivals and processions that developed with the spread of Christianity. Other pantomime precursors in Britain included the plays based on biblical stories that were originally performed in Latin by members of the Church. These were transformed during the 13th century by groups of secular actors who performed in English. They acted out what became known as mystery cycles and miracle plays in non-church premises and often in the streets. Gradually these plays became less religious and more satirical in nature. Despite being 'outside' the Church, the performance of such plays still fell victim to the anti-Catholic and Puritanical purges of the 16th and 17th centuries.

Another medieval midwinter entertainment was that of mumming, performed, in silence, by groups of masked people. Such performances may have evolved from much earlier pagan winter ceremonies, but by the 12th century the masked play had been elevated to become part of the Christmas celebrations at Court. The mummers' play was also very much a village entertainment that evolved into a set plot involving characters such as St George who fights a non-Christian knight, and a doctor who revives the slain combatant. Even Father Christmas had a part, as did a male character dressed in women's clothes. The storylines were very much about death, resurrection and the triumph of good over evil.

During the 16th century, a novel form of entertainment developed in Italy and spread through France and into Britain. This was the *commedia dell'arte* (comedy of art), and parts of it were absorbed into the courtly Christmas masques of the 16th and 17th

THE CHRISTMAS MUMMERS

centuries. These involved gorgeous costumes, elaborate masks and clever scenery. In Elizabethan times they took the form of 'dumb-shows' but by the reign of James

I they were performed to a metrical dialogue. Some performances cost thousands of pounds to stage and involved eminent poets, musicians and architects. The scenery became very complex, as is evident from the description, quoted by Dawson (1902), of one early 17th-century masque:

> ... the scene was divided into two parts from the roof to the floor ... On the left a cave, and on the right a thicket from which issued Orpheus. At the back of the scene, at the sudden fall of a curtain, the upper part broke on the spectators, a heaven of clouds of all hues; the stars suddenly vanished, the clouds dispersed; an element of artificial fire played about the house ...

When the comedy of art was first introduced to the British public, the actors were mostly travelling French troupes that played out their comic pieces with a certain amount of improvisation. Not speaking English, the actors relied on mime, song and dance. Typically the story involved the hero Harlequin who is thwarted in his love for Columbine by her overprotective father, Pantaloon. Other characters included Pierrot, Clown and the father's servant Pulchinello. These performances later developed into the very popular 'Italian night scenes' which included comic chases that later evolved into the slapstick of both pantomime and circus.

The undisputed father of modern pantomime was

John Rich. From his parents he inherited a share in Lincoln's Inn Fields Theatre in 1714. Eighteen years later he founded Covent Garden Theatre. Under his stage name of Lun, John brought financial rewards to both theatres through his playing the part of Harlequin in what were billed as ballet-pantomimes, more commonly known as harlequinades. The success of these productions that were offered throughout the year prompted his great rival David Garrick to produce 'pantomimes' at his Theatre Royal in Drury Lane. Garrick's pantomimes differed in that the performances included spoken parts.

By the end of the 18th century, a night at the theatre often involved the performance of several shows, the harlequinades being offered as short pieces at the end of the evening. Meanwhile the pantomime itself was developing as a mixture of the harlequinade, mystery play, masque and old folk/fairy tales. The 1773 performance of *Jack the Giant Killer* at the Theatre Royal was perhaps the earliest pantomime with a story comparable to our modern shows. In 1781 the newly written *Robinson Crusoe* still included Harlequin and Pantaloon as central characters. Many of the favourite pantomime titles that are still with us today were initiated towards the end of the 18th and in the first decade of the 19th centuries. These included *Aladdin*, *Babes in the Wood*, *Mother Goose* and *Cinderella*.

The tradition of the court jester and the importance of buffoonery and slapstick (all ingredients of many Shakespearean plays) lived on through the part of the

Clown. In the early 19th century this role was most brilliantly played by the great Joseph Grimaldi. He made his name in *Mother Goose* in 1806 and among his admirers was the young Charles Dickens '[Grimaldi] ... in whose honour I am informed I clapped my hands with great precocity'. Grimaldi also played female roles and helped to initiate the role of the Pantomime Dame.

Such cross-dressing has a long pedigree. As part of the Roman winter Saturnalia festival men would dress in women's clothes and later, during the pre-Reformation development of theatre, when acting was not considered an appropriate life for women, female roles were taken by boys. Shakespeare's *Twelfth Night* revolves round cross-dressing, with Viola dressing as a young boy and later being mistaken for her brother Sebastian — the fact that the part would have been played by a boy just added to the confusion.

In Victorian times music-hall stars were frequently chosen to play the role of the Pantomime Dame. The casting of stars from other areas of the entertainment business in pantomime's leading roles has continued to this day. Pantomime also borrowed another music-hall tradition, that of the Principal Boy. Here the role of a young man is played by a young woman, whose costume enables her to show off at least the lower parts of her legs. This certainly went down well with the men in the audience, at a time when few

IN VICTORIAN TIMES MUSIC-HALL STARS WERE FREQUENTLY CHOSEN TO PLAY THE ROLE OF THE PANTOMIME DAME.

women from upper-and middle-class society revealed much more than their face in polite society.

While the Dame role remained firmly in male hands, the Principal Boy's role in the 20th century was played by both women and men – the latter (such as Cliff Richard) frequently being pop stars. Recently the likes of Melinda Messenger have played the Principal Boy, although in her case it may not have been her *legs* that enticed the dads to accompany the rest of the family to the pantomime ...

Pantomime today still bears many of the hallmarks of its predecessors, but as with any surviving art it has adapted with the times. Leading roles in modern pantomimes are filled with television soap stars, though sadly many lack the timing and intuitive skills that make a great pantomime performer. Satire is still an important feature, with members of the government and the Royal Family particularly at risk. Good still wins out over evil; improvisation, slapstick, song, dance and puns are all essential elements. So too are the catchphrases such as 'He's behind you' and 'Oh Yes it is'.

At the start of the new century pantomime no longer features in the West End where it originated. The all-important foreign tourists do not appreciate what has become a uniquely British form of Christmas entertainment. Fortunately, however, pantomime is flourishing in the provincial theatres. Charles Dickens (*Memoirs of Joseph Grimaldi*) writing of his own times, remarked: 'Pantomime ... kept its place in the bills of the patent theatres because of its role in the budget.

The profit on a successful production helped substantially to meet the frequent losses on literature, Shakespeare often included ...'

For many children, the Christmas pantomime is their first taste of live theatre, and as my own children, Martin and Bryony, have grown up they have enjoyed at least one pantomime every year in their home city of Sheffield. In addition to excellent professional pantomimes, Sheffield has long been the home of the country's largest amateur pantomime as performed by members of The Manor Operatic Society. Brian Platts excels as the Grand Dame, as he has done for over 30 years. The shows include spectacular sets, large choruses, great singing, acrobats, terrible puns and pastry throwing. The £250,000 costs are recouped by 24 sell-out performances at the 2,200-seat City Hall. All this is without the assistance of a single soap star and is a tribute to the continued need for *good* live family entertainment at Christmas.

As a finale I would add that in February 2002 my children attended another amateur pantomime in Sheffield, one that did include a star from another walk of life. This was our local MP, Richard Allen, who was a marvellous evil Sheriff in *Babes in the Wood*. Perhaps his success will see a new trend for the ever-changing pantomime, but I leave it to the reader to imagine those politicians best-suited to play the part of the Dame or the Principal Boy.

THE GOOSE IS GETTING FAT

A Not-so-fresh Flesh Fest

The overeating that has long been associated with Christmas originates from a fusion of ancient feasts, including those held as part of harvest and Yuletide festivities and the excesses of the Roman Saturnalia. More recent modifications to the Christmas fare have resulted from Victorian ideals and imports from the New World, together with changing tastes and fashions throughout the 20th century.

In the modern world, where out-of-season fresh food is imported from thousands of miles away and frozen food can be eaten at any season, it is easy to forget the constraints our ancestors had to contend with. Over much of Europe, late autumn and early winter marked the end of the harvest. (Modern crop varieties tend to mature much earlier.) It was also the time when many animals fattened on summer herbage and autumn fruits were killed off. This culling was necessitated by insufficient fodder and shelter to sustain more than a few animals through the winter. The culled animals were preserved (often with salt) to provide meat through the winter, but the slaughter dates were incorporated into feasts and rituals, when a surfeit of fresh meat preceded many months without it.

Scholars have reasoned that depending on the latitudes of various European countries (and the availability of winter fodder) the dates for the pagan harvest/slaughter festivals have varied. These range from around the winter solstice (or even the end of December) in the extreme south to earlier in December, through November or as early as the end of October in the far north. The modern Christmas, New Year, St Nicholas's Day (6 December), St Martin's Day (11 November) and Hallowe'en celebrations are all believed to be remnants of older harvest/slaughter festivals. The Romans from their Italian base in the south enjoyed their feasting (Saturnalia) towards the latter part of December, much later than the people of northern Europe.

The Pilgrim Fathers moved their feast time from Christmas (from their Puritan viewpoint it was considered both a pagan and a Catholic feast day) to a date towards the end of November as their Thanksgiving or harvest festival. The earlier onset of severe winter conditions on the eastern side of North America compared with the British winter may have influenced the bringing forward of the feast date. To the pre-Christian Celts, Scandinavian and Germanic Norse peoples, a feast was also a time for thanking the gods (sometimes with sacrifices) for the food that they had provided.

Chief among the gods to be thanked was Frey (from whom we take the day name Friday) and his twin sister Freya, the god and goddess of fertility. Frey's animal symbol was the boar and the sacrificing and eating of both wild and domestic pigs was a common theme to many of the festivals. Wild boar (*Sus scrofa*), which still exists in parts of mainland Europe including regions of Germany and Poland, was once common throughout much of northern Europe. It was only finally hunted to extinction in England during the time of Henry III and in Scotland during the 17th century.

Throughout the more northern parts of Europe, boar's head was a prized component of the harvest feasts and later became the meat to be eaten on Christmas Day. In Britain it was the food of royalty and noblemen who also enjoyed hunting the animal. In medieval England, ritual accompanied the serving of wild boar and it was serenaded on its way to the dining room by the sounds of trumpets and singing. The head was usually served with an orange between its teeth (representing the sun at a time close to the winter solstice) or a more readily accessible substitute in the form of an apple. Some believe that it was this custom that was the origin of serving apple-sauce with pork.

When the 17th-century Commonwealth Government

attempted to suppress Christmas, it was not only sales of pigs' heads that declined but also those of mustard, which was an important accompaniment to the dish.

WILD BOAR ARE MAKING SOMETHING OF A COMEBACK AND ARE NOW BEING FARMED IN BRITAIN FOR THEIR MEAT

Even with the Restoration, the eating of boar's head never regained its popularity (partly because it was almost extinct in Britain by this time), although it featured in many famous 19th-century illustrations as part of Victorian nostalgia for the Old Christmas.

Today, the closest most people get to boar's head at Christmas is the ham or bacon that is served with the turkey. The tradition still lingers on at Queen's College Oxford. There, since 1341, on the last Saturday before Christmas, a cooked boar's head, decorated with holly, mistletoe, rosemary and bay, is carried in on a silver dish in front of the Provost and fellows at the high-table while the choir sings 'The Boar's Head Carol'.

Wild boar are making something of a comeback and are now being farmed in Britain for their meat, which has a much more gamey flavour than pork. Wild boar meat has proved particularly popular at Christmas, though not always in the form of the head. Several animals have lived up to their name by escaping from captivity and, especially in Sussex and Dorset, there are now growing populations of truly wild boar.

Other traditional Christmas meats included saddle of mutton and various forms of game (venison, hare, rabbit, etc.) often served in a pie. Pressed ox tongue has long been part of the Christmas food. Eating fish at

Christmas was also very popular, especially salmon and carp. By Victorian times in England (especially in the north) roast beef, in the form of sirloin or a baron of beef, was the main red meat eaten at Christmas.

Gobblers, Guard Geese and Goose Grease

Birds have long featured on the menu for important feasts. Among those consumed in earlier times was the peacock. This was not plucked but skinned with the plumage kept intact. After roasting, the meat, daubed with saffron in melted butter, was put back into the skin, which was then sewn up. An alcohol-soaked wick placed in the beak was set alight as the dish was carried in. It was of course the male (peacock) that was used, as the female (peahen) lacks the incredible tail.

Swan, long the preserve of royalty in this country, was also served with much of its plumage intact. Other game birds include the native common partridge (*Perdix perdix*), the pheasant (*Phasianus colchicus*), introduced by the Romans, and the great bustard (*Otis tarda*), a huge, turkey-like bird that was hunted to extinction in 1845.

In Scotland the native capercaille (sometimes known as wild turkey) survived at least a century longer than it did in England. In 1617 James I (James VI of Scotland) wrote to his cousin Lord Tullibardine, suggesting that he should 'now and then send to us by way of present … the known commodite yee have to provide, capercaillies and … the rairitie of these foules will both make their estimation the more pretious'. Royalty seems to have precipitated the bird's demise as among the last-known birds were those featured in a watercolour at Balmoral Castle. This depicted two birds shot for a marriage feast in 1785.

The bird has since been reintroduced into Scotland, but after a relatively successful period is once again under threat of extinction with fewer than 1,000 birds remaining. This is blamed on the loss of its habitat and the fact that the birds are injured when they fly into deer fences. In 2001 it was placed on a list of protected species, to the dismay of many Scottish landowners who had profited from game shoots of what they described as more like a wood partridge, with a much richer taste than turkey.

By medieval times there was a plentiful supply of domestic fowls in the form of capons – castrated cockerels fattened specially for eating. However, the most traditional of all the Christmas birds is the goose, as featured in the old rhyme:

> Christmas is coming, the geese are getting fat,
> Please put a penny in the old man's hat.
> If you haven't got a penny a ha'penny will do,
> If you haven't got a ha'penny,
> God bless you.

While halfpennies, to give them their full title, are a thing of the past (and these were pre-decimalisation pennies) and few beggars of today would bless those without any change, geese (along with the colour supplements) are still getting fat for Christmas. When most of the population lived in rural settlements, even the poor were able to keep a few geese, where they served as effective burglar alarms before ending up on the table at Christmas. In addition to providing good food they were valued as suppliers of medicinal goose grease.

As more people moved to urban areas, geese were 'marched' from where they were bred in the country towards London and other big cities in time for Christmas. Sometimes the journeys took several months and at the edge of the cities the birds were rested and re-fattened before arriving at the markets. In Victorian times many poorer people belonged to goose clubs and by contributing small sums weekly from September onwards were able to afford the Christmas goose. Such was the demand that many birds were imported from France and Germany. The large ovens of local bakers were used by people who did not own a big enough stove in which to cook their festive bird.

On Christmas Eve 1588, Queen Elizabeth I is said to have been feasting on goose at Greenwich Palace when news reached her of the final destruction of the Spanish Armada. Ironically, it was the Spanish who were responsible for introducing the goose's main competitor to Europe. The turkey (*Meleagris gallopavo*) is native to the United States and eastern Mexico and was unknown in Europe before the exploits of the Spanish Conquistadors in the 16th century. In Mexico (c.1518)

the Spanish encountered turkeys in regions where they are still found wild today. The predominantly black-feathered bird lives for up to ten years and despite a weight of up to 5kg can fly at 60kph. The noise of its warning cry, 'turk – turk', is the most likely source of its name; it has no connection with Turkey. The females are known as hens but the larger males are called gobblers, after the wonderful noise that they make.

The local peoples had already domesticated the bird when the Spanish arrived and it was domestic stock that was brought back to Spain. Having reached Spain in the 1520s, turkeys were later introduced into the Netherlands (then under Spanish control) and from there over to England in the middle of the 16th century. An old rhyme, quoted by Sir Richard Baker (1568–1645), gives some indication of when that was:

Hops and Turkies, Carps and Beer,
Came into England all in a year.

The carp was another introduction from the New World via Europe and it too was to become a popular Christmas food. Unfortunately, poetic licence may have shortened the period when the new items arrived as the use of hops, for making beer rather than ale, apparently spread from Flanders in the early 1520s, some years before the turkey arrived. The most likely date for the turkey's introduction is about 1542 and this is in line with the belief that Henry VIII (who died in

1547) was the first monarch in England to eat turkey on Christmas Day.

An early account indicates that among the first birds to arrive was a consignment landed near Bridlington 'about 1550'. The rearing of turkeys became concentrated on East Anglia and there are records of birds being sold at markets in Suffolk by 1555. By the 17th century, turkey was becoming more popular, but only as a dish for the very wealthy. Following the interest shown by Henry

THE TURKEYS WERE WALKED TO LONDON IN MASS TURKEY 'DRIVES'. THE WEAR-AND-TEAR ON THEIR FEET WAS CONSIDERABLE AND THIS RESULTED IN THE PRACTICE OF 'SHOEING' THE TURKEYS WITH SACKING OR LEATHER.

VIII, the turkey continued to enjoy royal patronage and in the 18th century George II kept a large flock of the birds in Richmond Park.

By the time of George II turkeys were becoming cheaper but most birds were reared in Norfolk and Suffolk, somewhat farther from London's markets than Richmond Park. In a manner comparable to that described earlier for geese, the turkeys were walked to London in mass turkey 'drives'. As with geese the wear-and-tear on their feet was considerable and this resulted in the practice of 'shoeing' the turkeys with sacking or leather. Geese had always resisted this, hence the old saying 'as impossible as shoeing a goose'. The feet of geese were sometimes covered in tar as an alternative means of protection.

In Dickens' *A Christmas Carol* (1843), the Cratchit family prepared a goose:

Such a bustle ensued that you might have thought a goose the rarest of all birds … There never was such a goose … Its tenderness and flavour, size and cheapness, were the themes of universal admiration. Eked out by the apple-sauce and mashed potatoes, it was a sufficient dinner for the whole family.

After the three spirits had visited Scrooge, he purchased a turkey for the family: 'It was a turkey! He never could have stood upon his legs, that bird.'

Eight years after *A Christmas Carol* was first published, Queen Victoria and Prince Albert switched from swan to turkey on Christmas Day and this encouraged many of their subjects to switch from goose to turkey. As with Christmas trees and crackers the Royal Family was influential in the development of new Christmas customs. By the end of the 19th century, turkey had become the choice Christmas meat of the middle class and birds were transported to Smithfield and other markets in steam-driven drays.

The older turkey breeds, like those in the wild, had brown-black feathers. Bronze turkeys, originally from Hudson Bay, and breeds such as the Norfolk Black, especially when fattened 'free-range', are considered by connoisseurs to have a flavour worth paying extra for, but white-feathered breeds became the norm when factory farming was introduced after the Second World War. These birds are not only easier to pluck but give a cleaner-looking dressed bird, the others have more of a

5 o'clock shadow. The cheapness of such birds was to spread the turkey custom into poorer country homes where previously the goose had remained the mainstay of Christmas. At 28p a pound (about 67p a kilo) in 1995, turkey was cheaper than most dog food. By the end of the 20th century some 15 million turkeys were being sold in Britain each year, in the run-up to Christmas.

The king of the English turkey-breeders is Bernard Matthews, whose firm, based in Norfolk, sells millions of birds, not just for the Christmas market. At the age of 20 he bought 20 turkey eggs and a small incubator for a total of fifty shillings and after rearing the young for just four weeks he sold them for fifteen shillings each. He later went on to fill most of the 35 rooms of the then dilapidated Great Witchingham Hall (the firm's headquarters), before erecting turkey houses on disused airfields in the region. Mr Matthews initially concentrated on smaller birds that would fit in modern ovens. A very successful television advertising campaign showing him as a tweed-clad farmer, talking with his Norfolk accent, helped him to maintain a successful business for over 50 years.

As a child (before I gave up eating meat) I remember that the Christmas turkey carcass appeared for several more meals after its initial carving. Once the breast meat had all been finished two members of the family partook of an ancient custom, that of pulling the wishbone. The V-shaped bone near the breast (also present in other poultry) was removed and while one person held one end, with the other person on the opposite end, the bone was pulled apart until it broke. At this point the person with the longer piece made a silent wish. In some regions of Britain the bone was called the merry-thought and the person left holding the shorter piece gained the wish. The custom still continues, although it is under threat from boneless joints and turkey drummers.

In Britain turkey may be the most popular of the Christmas fowl but goose, duck and pheasant are still viable alternatives and provide a tastier meat. In America, turkey is indigenous and is an essential part of the Thanksgiving meal. Having chosen the Christmas meat, the next job of the cook is to provide all the stuffings, sauces and vegetables that will accompany it.

Of Stuffing, Sprouts and Cranberry Sauce

Almost as important as the choice of bird for the Christmas table is the stuffing, or forcemeat to give it its earlier name, that accompanies the poultry. Cynics argue that modern, shed-reared turkey needs a good stuffing to give it some taste, but additionally stuffing helps to retain the bird's shape and make the meat go further. Stuffing is also served with other meats and was even used in the roasting of wild boar. Recent research at Hampton Court has shown that the stuffing packed into the carcass was instrumental in keeping the animal firmly attached to the slender iron rod on which it was cooked.

Turkey meat can become very dry on cooking, and pork sausagemeat (or chopped streaky bacon) is a basic ingredient of stuffing as its fat helps to keep the turkey flesh moist. The other essential ingredients of a good stuffing were originally included for a very different reason, that of ensuring that the diners lasted beyond Boxing Day. In earlier centuries poultry was hung for longer as this improved both the texture and flavour. This, together with the absence of refrigeration, meant that food poisoning from a range of bacterial infections was a considerable risk, especially with an undercooked bird.

So most traditional stuffing contains some or all of the following ingredients: onion, sage, parsley, marjoram and thyme (or mixed herbs). Onion contains a range of volatile sulphide chemicals that are mildly antiseptic, thus helping to prevent infections of the digestive tract. In addition, onion lowers both blood pressure and cholesterol levels, so its effects help to undo some of the results of Christmas overeating.

Sage, marjoram and thyme all belong to the same family of plants (*Labiatae* or *Lamiaceae* to give it its modern name), characterised by a high content of volatile oils. These give the herbs not only their strong aroma but also their medicinal properties. The oils of marjoram and thyme are strongly antiseptic (thus working with onion to prevent infection) and together with those from sage also relieve flatulence by their carminative action. Essential oils in sage also reduce perspiration and so could be said to take the sweat out of Christmas.

Cranberries are another way of adding flavour as well as colour to a turkey meal. Cranberry (*Vaccinium oxycoccos*) is a rare native plant in Britain with delicate, thin stems that creep over the surface of sphagnum moss in boggy moorland. The tiny pink flowers are like miniature cyclamens and the red fruits are the size and shape of small peas, considerably smaller than those of the American cranberry (*Vaccinium macrocarpon*).

Wild cranberries were formerly more common, especially in northern England and Scotland where they were collected and sold in local markets. In the 19th century the berries were bottled and sold in London. Queen Victoria described a meal in 1868 at Balmoral Castle that ended with 'a good tart of cranberries'. Cranberry sauce was served as an accompaniment to venison long before turkeys were introduced to Britain.

By the 19th century the larger berries of the American species were already being imported into Britain. In their native land they had been part of the first turkey Thanksgiving feasts in New England during the 1620s. A little later in the 17th century German immigrants in America christened them 'kranbeeres', from the resemblance of the slender-stemmed pink flowers to the long-legged cranes that frequented the marshes where the plants grew.

Since the 1970s, fresh berries have been imported from the United States and towards the end of the 20th century, cranberry sauce was becoming a more common accompaniment to turkey than the more traditional bread sauce. As with some of the plant ingredients of stuffing, cranberries have useful medicinal properties and are especially good at alleviating cystitis. In 1995 Delia Smith used cranberries in no fewer than nine recipes in her best-selling cookery book *Winter Collection*. The book led to a 200 per cent increase in sales of cranberries during the weeks before Christmas and many suppliers ran short. Reputedly stocks were high in one supermarket chain (Sainsbury's), which was helped by having Delia's husband on its payroll.

DELIA SMITH USED CRANBERRIES IN NO FEWER THAN NINE RECIPES IN HER BEST-SELLING COOKERY BOOK <u>WINTER COLLECTION</u>. THE BOOK LED TO A 200 PER CENT INCREASE IN SALES OF CRANBERRIES DURING THE WEEKS BEFORE CHRISTMAS.

In addition to roast potatoes, the vegetable accompaniment to the Christmas meat has long been the Brussels sprout. The origin of this cabbage relative possibly dates back to the 5th century, though it appears not to have reached Britain until the 16th century, about the same time as the turkey. During the 19th century, Brussels sprouts became synonymous with Christmas in an age when children probably had to eat them, regardless of the flavour. The rather bitter-tasting vegetables are not best-loved by the average British child (or indeed many adults), which is a pity as they are rich in antioxidant flavonoids that have been closely linked with the prevention of cancer.

The Christmas meal has always been one of many courses and the main course is traditionally high in saturated fats and calories. Many of the dishes that follow do little to restore the balance.

Mince Pies, Cake and Lies about Liking Pudding

Many of the foods now looked on as constituents of the sweet course at Christmas started life containing meat and as part of the main course. Nowhere is this more evident than with the plum pudding, aka Christmas pudding. The likely forerunner of this was plum pottage, also known as plum porridge. This included a broth of beef and mutton, thickened with breadcrumbs to which wine, spices and dried fruit were added, the latter including raisins and prunes (dried plums). It had a consistency more like that of thin porridge and was eaten with, or even before, the meat course.

A similar dish known as frumenty (or furmety) consisted of hulled wheat boiled in milk, with added eggs, sugar and spices such as cinnamon. Christmas puddings also owe their origin to the bag puddings that were popular in medieval times. These were cooked in a skin (like the original black puddings and haggis), which was replaced by flannel or cloth in the Elizabethan period, just as the prune was becoming popular.

Plum pottage and frumenty had largely been replaced by the more solid plum pudding (eaten after the meat course) by the beginning of the Victorian era, though by then plum puddings had been around (and a round shape) for over 200 years. In the mid-17th century the Puritans declared Christmas pudding a 'lewd custom unfit for God-fearing people', but the dish survived. Later King George I (also known as the Pudding King) enjoyed a particularly rich plum pudding at 6am on the occasion of his first Christmas Day in England in 1714. In addition to the dried plums, this included suet (but no meat), eggs, milk, flour, breadcrumbs, sugar, peel, raisins, sultanas, currants, spices and a very liberal glassful of brandy. Cynics regarded his show of eating the pudding with relish as a publicity stunt, designed to show his liking for English food despite his German ancestry.

Making a Christmas pudding still involves steaming the ingredients for many hours. In the past, puddings were also reheated by steaming, but microwave ovens make the task much simpler. As a child who grew up in the 1950s, I can still remember the strange smells emanating from the cloth-wrapped pudding as it steamed away for hours on the stove at Christmas. By then the pudding had a flat bottom, one of the few changes from the cannon-ball shape of earlier times. The smell was vividly described by Dickens in *A Christmas Carol*, as he captured the scene in the Cratchits' kitchen:

A smell like a washing day! That was the cloth. A smell like an eating-house and a pastrycook's next door to each other, with a laundress's next door to that! That was the pudding!

These days, fewer than 20 per cent of families sit down to a homemade Christmas pudding. In a recent poll, 35 per cent of people interviewed admitted that they did not like Christmas pudding and even when it is served (an estimate puts the number at 40 million puddings eaten at Christmas) a lot tends to get left on the plate. Many people now buy ready-made puddings and one factory in Derbyshire, owned by Northern Foods, produces 20 million puddings a year.

Of the many different recipes, some now exclude the suet so that the pudding is suitable for the growing band of vegetarians. Others are advertised as low fat (a medium portion of a normal pudding provides at least 250 calories, while cream or brandy butter adds about a further 100 calories). Some are even alcohol-free to the chagrin of many. At home, foil has largely replaced cloth in the heating process, but the customary sprig of holly is still stuck on top of the pudding. For the best visual effect, brandy is poured over the pudding and ignited just before it is carried into the dining room.

THESE DAYS, FEWER THAN 20 PER CENT OF FAMILIES SIT DOWN TO A HOMEMADE CHRISTMAS PUDDING.

For those who still make their own puddings, the well-organised cook does so some weeks before Christmas. This is because, like a good whisky, the longer it matures, the better it tastes, and there is enough to do on Christmas morning without having to cook the pudding. Traditionally the pudding should be made on the last Sunday before Advent. This is known as Stir-Up Sunday but the name actually originates from the church collect for the day 'Stir up, we beseech Thee, O Lord, the wills of thy faithful people'. All of the family should be involved with the stirring, and on their turn each person is supposed to make a secret wish. Purists make sure that the direction of the stirring is from east to west, to remind them of the direction travelled by the wise men on their way to Bethlehem.

My childhood memories also left me with a cautious approach to the eating of Christmas pudding. This was to avoid swallowing the sixpenny piece that was slipped into the pudding and supposed to bring the finder good luck. My mother always managed to ensure that I found, but did not swallow, one of the small silver coins. I only discovered later that this was a throwback to a much earlier custom when the Lord of Misrule (a sort of director of festivities) was chosen by similar means.

From medieval times a special cake eaten on Twelfth Night included a bean, the finder of which became the Bean King (a sort of one-day version of the Lord of Misrule). In Victorian times the Twelfth Night cake (and the rather boisterous events that followed its consumption) was transformed into the more sedate rich-fruit Christmas cake. This was covered with almond paste, better known as marzipan, that prevented the white icing from being stained by the underlying fruit cake. In parts of France the *galette des rois* (Twelfth Night cake) is still made and this includes almond paste, as does stollen, a German cake served at Christmas.

Like plum puddings, mince pies started life as a meat dish. Originally these Christmas pies were much larger than their modern counterpart, and of a narrow, oval shape, closer to that of a manger. The earliest mention of these shred or shrid pies (the term comes from the shredded meat contents) is in 1557 and even by the 17th century they were much more of a savoury dish, filled with beef (and its suet) together with rosewater, cinnamon, nutmeg, apples, orange peel, dates and currants. The expensive spices were representative of the gifts presented by the Magi.

Minced pies, as they became known, were banned by Cromwell in the Puritan purge during the 17th century. Although they surfaced again with the Restoration, they did so in a style more similar to the smaller, rounder tarts of today. In this form they were often offered to visitors and called wayfarers' pies. Further changes took place during the Victorian period and, by the end of the 19th century, meat was no longer included, although the suet was kept in to help preserve the mixture. Even the suet has been largely replaced in modern, commercially produced mince pies where sugar is now the principal preservative. What was once a savoury pie has become a very sweet one.

Folklore with regard to mince pies includes the belief that eating at least one mince pie on each of the Twelve Days of Christmas will ensure a year ahead with twelve happy and healthy (if slightly overweight) months. When the mince pie was still a form of meat pie there were other pies that contained as many as a dozen different meats, including goose, snipe, blackbird and rabbit. It is this sort of pie that is alluded to in the well-known rhyme:

> Little Jack Horner
> Sat in a corner
> Eating a Christmas Pie
>
> He put in his thumb
> And pulled out a plum
> And said 'what a good boy am I'.

Some authors have taken the plum (or prune) at face value, but it is more likely to mean plum in the sense of 'the best'. The rhyme dates from the 16th century, a time when Henry VIII was restricting the power of the Catholic Church. By 1539 Glastonbury Abbey was one of the few religious houses untouched by this purge. This may have been because of the influence of the Glastonbury thorn (see page 236), but is more likely to be because the then Abbot of Glastonbury, one Richard Whiting, had attempted to curry favour by sending Christmas gifts to the king.

The final Christmas gift from Whiting is said to have been a pie with the pie-crust strongly attached to the pie-container and sent to London under the watchful eye of Whiting's steward, Mr Thomas Horner. Given the transport system of the time the journey probably took at least four days and this was plenty of time for

Thomas to investigate the pie. The story goes that underneath the pie-crust were a dozen sets of deeds to the richest manors belonging to the Abbey. Being the steward, Thomas knew which was the best of these and took the 'plum' – the manor at Mells. On reaching London, Horner is said to have got on very well with the king and later became a member of the 'complaisant jury' that tried and condemned, among others, his former boss Abbot Whiting.

An old saying in Somerset hints at this story:

Hopton, Horner, Smyth and Thynne,
When Abbots went out, they came in.

Why then does the more well-known poem refer to him not as Thomas but Jack Horner? The answer might be tied up with a fear of litigation, but is more likely to be because a 'jack' was the equivalent of a knave, and that is what the locals accused Horner of being. At about this time the manor at Mells did indeed change hands, and records show that the new owners were called Horner. The family claims that the manor was purchased in a perfectly legal manner, but as loyal supporters of Henry VIII, the suspicion remains that even if not stolen from the pie, the estate was a present (for being a good boy) from the king.

Other 19th-century Christmas food included sweetmeats, nuts, oranges and gingerbread. The latter has now been replaced by the sponge-based Yule log. Nuts and oranges (now available as different hybrids such as clementines and the mandarin-like satsuma) remain popular but, now that they are available over a much longer season, are less specifically a Christmas treat. Dried fruits have long been the ingredients of Christmas food, as have dates from the Middle East. Towards the end of the 20th century, stollen (a cross between bread and cake) became another German tradition to be assimilated into the ever-changing British Christmas.

The Christmas Spirit

Alcohol, especially in the form of wine or beer, has been around for at least 5,000 years, and recent analysis of deposits found in ancient jars in Iran appear to show that wine has been with us for more like 7,000 years. The Roman Saturnalia midwinter festival was renowned for its drunkenness, while a similar overindulgence in alcohol was a feature of the more northern people's Yuletide celebrations.

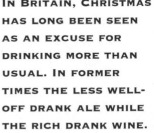

IN BRITAIN, CHRISTMAS HAS LONG BEEN SEEN AS AN EXCUSE FOR DRINKING MORE THAN USUAL. IN FORMER TIMES THE LESS WELL-OFF DRANK ALE WHILE THE RICH DRANK WINE.

In Britain, Christmas has long been seen as an excuse for drinking more than usual. In former times the less well-off drank ale (as it was known before the 16th-century introduction of hops that gave us a more bitter beer) while the rich drank wine. Given the coldness of the season many Christmas drinks were served hot, especially when drunk by those such as outdoor carol singers who were exposed to the elements.

In former times the communal wassail-bowl was passed round in a shared drinking ceremony. Wassail comes from two Anglo-Saxon words, *was hael* (Old English wes hal), meaning 'be thou hale' or 'be well'. The cry of 'wassail' has now been replaced by the more modern 'good health' or simply 'cheers'. The contents of the bowl varied in different parts of the country, but a popular one was known as lambswool. It consisted of hot ale (or beer), eggs, sugar, cream, spices and (as Shakespeare described it) 'roasted crabs hiss in the bowl'. The latter were roasted crab-apples, not sea food. Pieces of bread or toast were also included in the drink, the person getting the toast being deemed lucky. This may be why we now 'drink a toast' to wish someone well. In parts of Wales the mix of cakes, apples and spices came out more like a wet, very alcoholic trifle.

Another festive drink was posset. This was based on hot milk with either ale or wine together with sugar, lemon and spices. Traditionally it was drunk on Christmas Eve from a two-handled pot. Some possets contained raw eggs and the egg-nog (advocaat) is a modern form of these so-called comfort drinks.

In 1830 the Prime Minister removed the tax on beer and cider in an attempt to reduce the consumption of gin. The distillers responded by opening gin palaces, the equivalent of the theme pub of today, and drink became a major problem, especially among the urban working classes of Victorian Britain. The better off, as represented by Mr Pickwick, had a wider choice, including port, sherry and spirits such as whisky and brandy. On one occasion Mr Pickwick recollected 'having taken something stronger than exercise on the previous night' and Mrs Sparsit (*Hard Times*) recommended the drinking of warm sherry with lemon-peel and nutmeg.

In fact, the hot punch popular in Victorian times, and with us today as mulled wine, is a more modern version of the wassail drink. A form of mulled wine appears in *A Christmas Carol* when Scrooge proposes that he and Bob Cratchit share some 'Smoking Bishop'. At the time such drinks were probably safer to drink than much of the water.

Towards the end of Victoria's reign George Bernard Shaw provided a deeply cynical view of Christmas in *Music in London 1890–1894*: 'Like all intelligent people, I greatly dislike Christmas ... We must be gluttonous because it is Christmas. We must be drunken because it is Christmas.'

Wassail also appears in another form at Christmas, namely in the wassailing of fruit trees. This ancient custom is derived from the ancient fertility rites associated with the pagan winter solstice festival and the desire to drive away evil spirits said to be at their most dangerous at this time of year. Wassailing is still performed in a few places, especially in the west of England. Typically it used to take place on Twelfth Night, though in Somerset, where the flowering of the

Glastonbury thorn did not fit well with the new calendar, it was often performed on Old Twelfth Night (now 17 January). As darkness fell, the orchards were blessed by sprinkling cider on the roots of a chosen tree, while toast soaked in cider was placed on the branches and a great deal of noise was made (sometimes by firing shotguns) 'to drive away evil spirits from the trees'. Songs were sung to encourage the productivity of the orchard and a great deal of mulled cider was consumed.

The Devon poet Robert Herrick wrote:

Wassail the trees that they may beare
You many a Plum and many a peare:
For more or less Fruits they will bring,
As you doe give them Wassailing.

Today, twice as much alcohol (and 30 per cent of the annual sales of Scotch whisky) is sold in the three months of October, November and December as in any other quarter. Around 90 per cent of men and 80 per cent of women will drink alcohol in one form or another over the Christmas period. One unhappy result of this is the increased number of drink-related traffic accidents during the festive period. A modern Christmas custom is the annual advertising campaign warning drivers of the potential dangers of mixing drinking and driving.

Even Santa Claus is depicted as being a little merry and rather too many people suffer the ignominy of friends declaring them to be 'getting pissed'. Despite the fact that the diuretic effect of alcohol greatly increases the quantity of urine (by considerably more than the amount of liquid consumed), the term 'getting pissed' was not originally connected with alcohol. Santa may well have got pissed but, as explained on page 106, the imbibed liquid was far from alcoholic.

OTHER CHRISTMAS QUIRKS AND QUERIES

Early Mornings, Holly Floggings and First Footers

No attempt has been made here to cover the many local Christmas customs that used to occur in villages and small communities all over the British Isles. Instead, this book is about national customs and widely held practices. It is, however, useful to outline briefly how some Welsh Christmas traditions evolved as separate customs to those found in England.

Plygain

This Welsh service has its origin in pre-Reformation times when the term described an ordinary morning service. Following the Reformation *plygain* meant a form of Protestant carol service held in the early hours of Christmas morning, when it replaced the more

Catholic-linked midnight mass. The service survived the rise of the nonconformist Chapel movement, but by the end of the 19th century it had ceased to be a widespread Welsh custom. In a few places *plygain* survived with little or no break and the service is now being revived in other districts of Wales.

There was considerable variation in the timing (typically beginning at 3am but also as late as 5 or 6am) and form of service, which did not always include a sermon. Candles played an important role. Carols were the main feature of the service and these were sung in Welsh by soloists, duets, families and larger groups. Newly written carols were an important feature, along with old favourites, many written in the traditional metre. Typically the singing was unaccompanied – the tradition is vocal, not instrumental, and anything up to 30 carols might be aired during a service that could last for up to three hours.

The hours before the service were spent, by the younger people at least, putting up holly and ivy in the houses and making *cyflaith* (a sort of treacle toffee); there was also merrymaking in the streets. After the service feasting began in earnest with a special breakfast of hot ale, bread and cheese or cakes. People visited the homes of friends or relatives before returning home for the traditional Christmas dinner (lunch), of which goose was the favourite meat. Hunting of animals such as squirrel and rabbit, and rather loose games of football were all part of the sociable, outdoor Christmas Day celebrations, which gave way in Victorian times to the quieter, mostly indoor, family day.

Boxing Day

In parts of Wales, 26 December was commemorated by a strange custom that was only finally outlawed in Victorian times. Holly beating or holming, as it was known in some areas, took the form of men and boys beating the unclothed arms of women servants (or other women considered to be of a lower class) with holly branches, until their arms bled. This may have been originally linked to the practice, on the same day, of bleeding horses and other animals; it being thought that this improved their health. A more probable explanation for the beating is the link with the first Christian martyr St Stephen, whose feast day this is.

HOLLY BEATING OR HOLMING, AS IT WAS KNOWN IN SOME AREAS, TOOK THE FORM OF MEN AND BOYS BEATING THE UNCLOTHED ARMS OF WOMEN SERVANTS WITH HOLLY BRANCHES, UNTIL THEIR ARMS BLED.

Hunting the Wren

In Wales the robin is not the only small bird to be associated with Christmas. As in other Celtic countries, rituals involving the wren were commonplace. The Hunting of the Wren traditionally took place over the midwinter period. After a wren had been caught, it was usually killed and carried round on a pole decorated with holly leaves. This pre-Christian custom was later linked (like the holly beating) to the feast of St

Stephen. This came from a story which told of when Stephen had tried to escape from his Roman captors and the sleeping guard had been alerted by the alarm call of a wren. On Twelfth Night a dead (or imprisoned) wren was also carried by wassailers, inside a specially built wren house.

Those bearing the house would pretend that it was very heavy and would beg for money and drink. They would also sing songs, some of which featured the wren. In many of these songs the wren was looked on as the king of birds, a definite role-reversal for one of our smallest birds and thus reminiscent of the Lord of Misrule and Boy Bishop customs. The party concentrated on visiting newly married couples and some see this as the remnants of old fertility rites, the wren invoking the promise of a large brood.

New Year's Eve and New Year's Day

As in Scotland, the events surrounding the New Year were for a long time more important in Wales than was Christmas Day itself. The sex, hair colour and even initial letter of the name of the first visitor to a house after midnight on 31 December were crucial to the supposed future fortunes of the inhabitants. Some hours after the 'first footers', boys would visit houses to sprinkle rooms and inhabitants with water, in return for money.

Until the giving of Christmas presents became fashionable in the later years of the 19th century, the Welsh custom was to give gifts at New Year. Early 19th-century accounts tell of how, on the morning of

New Year's Day, children would visit houses to wish the inhabitants good health and fortune in the coming year. The children carried an apple (or orange in some areas) studded with corn, raisins, cloves and evergreens. The fruit was held by an inserted stick and three smaller sticks formed a tripod for putting it down safely. The children usually sang a verse or two of a carol in return for gifts (*calennig*) of money, fruit or *cyflaith*. Elements of the custom still continue in a few country areas and some recent church Nativity services in Wales include displays of cloved oranges on three sticks, with the addition of a candle on top.

Twelfth Night

Other Welsh traditions, common until 100 years ago, were closely linked with Twelfth Night (page 48) though not restricted to that occasion. The *Mari Lwyd* custom involved a party of wassail-singers including one carrying a horse's skull at the top of a pole. The man was hidden beneath a sheet and was able to operate a lever that caused the lower jaw of the horse to snap shut. On being admitted to a house, after a singing competition between the wassailers and the household, the 'grey mare', as it was also known, would snap and chase children and especially any women present. Finally the visiting party would be given food and drink.

As in England the calendar change introduced in 1752 caused much confusion in Wales and the moving of customs previously linked with New Year or Old

Christmas Day. Throughout the 19th century, 6 January (Twelfth Day) was also Old Christmas Day and it is possible that customs held on 6 January were originally part of Christmas Day celebrations. In parts of Wales Old New Year's Day (*Hen Galen*) is still celebrated (this is now on 13 January) in place of the current New Year's Day. In the early 19th century many of the parties held by farmers for those who had helped with the harvest were moved from 1 January to *Hen Galen*.

The Trouble with the Glastonbury Thorn

One of the most interesting Christmas legends concerns an unusual hawthorn that featured on the 13p Christmas stamp in 1986. Hawthorn (*Crataegus monogyna*) is a thorny, deciduous shrub or small tree and is also known as may. It is common in British woods, scrub-land and especially hedges, where millions of cuttings were planted as a result of the parliamentary enclosure acts of the 18th and 19th centuries.

The leaves typically emerge in April, but depending on the plant's location the flat-topped flower clusters open from as early as late April to as late as the end of June. The sickly, sweet smell of the flowers is tainted by the presence of triethylamine, a chemical more commonly associated with decaying flesh. The clusters of berries (haws) ripen from green to crimson through the late summer and remain on the tree after the leaves have dropped in the autumn. Along with the berries of holly, ivy and mistletoe, they provide winter food for birds and other animals.

There are probably more stories, legends, sacred sites and superstitions associated with hawthorn than with any other native British tree. Because of its red berries it has been looked on as a tree that brings good luck and provides protection (especially against witches). For these reasons sprigs were carried by wedding guests in Ancient Greece, and in Britain leafy branches were once hung above cradles. Conversely, many people thought that bringing the flowers into the house brought bad luck. Apart from the obnoxious smell, this fear is possibly due to the symbolic association with the may blossom and the Virgin Mary. During the years when Catholics were persecuted for their faith some are believed to have been betrayed by the presence of flowering hawthorn in their houses.

Hawthorn's alternative name of may comes partly from the fact that this is the month when it normally flowers but, more importantly, it is a reminder of the significant role played by its flowering branches in the May Day ceremony. In the Druids' calendar 1 May (Beltane) was the start of summer when the maypole (topped with hawthorn) symbolised the rebirth of the year. That hawthorn flowers were involved in what was a fertility rite is perhaps not surprising given that their smell has been compared to that of human semen. It is little wonder that the Puritans so disliked the plant.

As those from the more northerly parts of Britain will

know, it is often impossible to find hawthorn in flower as early as 1 May, so how can it have been such an important part of the May Day celebrations? The answer to this conundrum takes us back to problems with the calendar that were also to influence the *Christmas* flowering date of a very famous hawthorn known as the Glastonbury thorn, the one depicted on the Christmas stamp.

As has already been explained the Julian calendar assumed that the length of a year was 365¼ days. This was an overestimate, compared with astronomical measurements of the average length of the solar year, of almost 11 minutes or about one whole day every 128 years. This created a special problem for most branches of the Christian Church that, since the Nicaean Council in AD 325, had calculated the important date of Easter with reference to the spring equinox.

Many hundreds of years after Nicaea, the Julian calendar's reckoning of the spring equinox was some days *ahead* of the true astronomical equinox, resulting in inaccurate calculations for the Easter date. In the late 16th century, the Catholic Church under Pope Gregory decided to tackle this problem. By 1582, some 1257 years after Nicaea, the Julian calendar date was nearly ten days in advance of the equinox (one day in 128 years, ten days in 1280 years). So it was necessary to cut ten days from the calendar to restore the season of the spring equinox to where it had been at the time of the Nicaean Council.

In addition to restoring the calendar to its alignment

with the seasons any new calendar needed to include adjustments to account for the true length of the solar year. Pope Gregory chose Dr Lilius to sort out these calendar problems. He achieved this by fine-tuning the leap year rules. Working with a slightly different estimate of the length of a 'true' year giving a figure of one day to be lost every 134 years, Lilius rounded this to three days in 400 years. He proposed losing the three days by the cancelling of a leap year in three out of four 'century years', with only those divisible by 400 keeping the leap year. Thus, 1600 was to be a leap year in what became known as the Gregorian calendar, but not 1700, 1800 or 1900. (All 'century years' are leap years in the Julian calendar, as all are divisible by four.)

A Papal Bull issued by Pope Gregory 'eliminated' the ten days of 5 to 14 October 1582 and 4 October was followed by 15 October. In addition, the Roman New Year date of 1 January was chosen as standard, a change for those countries that had started their New Year from the old calendar's reckoning of the spring equinox, on 25 March. This was also the Annunciation date when the Archangel Gabriel announced that Mary was to bear the infant Jesus; another reason for making it the start of the year. Following Gregory's instructions, only the Catholic countries of Italy, Spain and Portugal changed to the Gregorian calendar in October 1582.

Many powerful figures in Britain dubbed the innovative calendar 'a Catholic plot' and, although Queen Elizabeth was surprisingly in favour of making the change, this was prevented by the then Archbishop of Canterbury. Subsequently, the Puritans and the Church of England blocked further attempts to convert to the new calendar. Britain finally made the change in 1752, some 170 years after the Papal Bull. (As I write this there is an obvious analogy with the current debate in Britain over whether to change to the common currency now used by other European countries.)

By 1752 the difference between the two calendars was more than ten days. The year 1600 was a leap year in both calendars, but the year 1700 had been observed under the Julian calendar as a leap year while those countries following the Gregorian calendar had not added a day in February. Accordingly when Britain finally made the change it did so by a government bill that resulted in the day after 2 September 1752 becoming 14 September. This action resulted in the plea to 'Give us back our eleven days'. At the same time, 1 January became the official start to the year (many people, including tax collectors had previously used 25 March). More to the point, 1 May 1753 now occurred eleven days *earlier* in relation to the solar year than it had been in previous years and over many parts of the country hawthorn was only in bud by May Day.

In Glastonbury, problems caused by the calendar change arrived towards the end of 1752, with the celebration of Christmas some eleven days earlier than it would have been under the old calendar (though it was still of course celebrated on 25 December). Glastonbury had already become famous as the home of a number of very unusual hawthorn trees, which in addition to flowering in May flowered for a second time at Christmas.

Before attempting to separate fact from legend in the story of the Glastonbury thorn it is worth noting what happened on Christmas Eve 1752 when, as was the usual custom, a crowd gathered to see whether one of the trees would produce flowers in time for Christmas. The buds, however, remained unopened. On returning 11 days later, on 'Old Christmas Eve' (4 January), the flowers were found to be open. As a result many people in the area continued to keep 'Old Christmas' on 5 January (when it was 25 December, according to the Julian calendar).

Some communities in Britain (including those on the Island of Foula and in the Gwaun Valley in Wales) and in other parts of the world (for example the Eastern Orthodox Church in Russia) still celebrate 'Old Christmas' by the Julian calendar. Between 1800 and 1899 this was 12 days later and conveniently coincided with Epiphany on 6 January. Since 1900 (and there was no further change in 2000 as this is divisible by both four and 400 and was a leap year in both calendars) the date has been 7 January. The range of dates (4 to 7 January) for 'Old Christmas' depends on the year in question. Lack of understanding of the link between the two calendars has led to the repeated quoting of inaccurate dates, especially when authors wrongly assume that the date given in a much older book will still apply today.

It is believed by many that Joseph of Arimathaea (the owner of the tomb where Christ's body lay for three days) came to Britain shortly after the crucifixion, to spread the gospel of Christianity. With eleven followers he arrived at Glastonbury, which at that time would have been a haven of dry land in the low-lying marshy region now known as the Somerset levels. Joseph carried a staff supposedly made from a hawthorn that had originated from Christ's crown of thorns. When the tired group arrived in Glastonbury, Joseph stuck his staff in the ground at the place where they were to spend the night (a spot now known as Wearyall Hill) and the staff immediately took root, sent out leafy branches and produced white blossoms.

This miracle is said by some to have occurred on Christmas Day and to have encouraged Joseph to settle and found a church in Glastonbury. There are stories in many parts of the world of trees (and other plants) coming into blossom on Christmas Day. Equally, there are other accounts of the blossoming of staffs, including one in the Old Testament:

> And Moses spake unto the children of Israel,
> And every one of their princes gave him
> a rod apiece,
> For each prince one,
> According to their fathers' houses,
> Even twelve rods:
> And the rod of Aaron was among their rods.

And Moses laid up the rods before the Lord in the tabernacle of witness.

And it came to pass, that on the morrow
Moses went into the tabernacle of witness;
And, behold, the rod of Aaron for the house of
Levi was budded,
And brought forth buds, and bloomed
blossoms, and yielded almonds.

(Numbers 17: 6–8)

There are less substantiated reports of another tree in Glastonbury, a miraculous walnut (also said to have grown from a staff of Joseph) that budded on 11 June (St Barnabas's Day). Perhaps the walnut was the closest the British could get to the almond mentioned in the above verses, as almonds infreqently yield mature fruits in the British Isles.

The earliest verbal account of a hawthorn flowering at Christmas comes not from Glastonbury but from Appleton in Cheshire, where there is a midsummer tradition of dressing a special hawthorn ('bawming' the thorn). The original Appleton thorn is said to have been planted by a returning Crusader in 1125. The thorn is reputed to have been a grafted cutting taken from one of the Glastonbury trees.

The first definitive written record of the Glastonbury trees (three on Wearyall Hill) appears nearly 400 years later in an anonymous poem, *Here*

begynneth the Lyfe of Joseph of Arimathia, published in 1520. The trees:

> Do burge and bere grene leaues at Christmas
> As fresihe as other in May when ye nightingale
> Wrestes out her notes musycall as pure glas.

It should be noted that the poem only credits the plant with leaves at Christmas; the unseasonal *flowering* was not written about until 1535. Cynics have observed that it was then that the Abbey at Glastonbury needed a miracle, though even this failed to prevent its suppression by Henry VIII. Despite this, the trees attracted considerable national attention for the rest of the 16th century and into the 17th century. Many local merchants cashed in by selling grafted cuttings of the trees.

During this time the custom of sending budded branches to the reigning monarch began. There is an amusing anecdote concerning Charles I who, on being handed a branch, was informed that 'the miracle was regarded with great veneration by Catholics'. By this time Rome had instigated the new Gregorian calendar, but Britain still stuck with the Julian system (old style). The king enquired whether the tree flowered on Christmas Day old style. On being told that it did, he joked 'the Pope and your miracle differ not a little, for he always celebrates Christmas Day ten days earlier by the calendar of new style ...'

In the middle of the 17th century, Cromwell rooted

out what was considered to be pagan or papal idolatry. Not only was the custom of sending a spray of Glastonbury thorn to the monarch abruptly stopped (as was the monarchy), but the surviving tree on Wearyall Hill is reputed to have been cut down by a Roundhead. The Bishop of Gloucester, writing in 1653 reported 'The White Thorn at Glastonbury which did usually blossome on Christmas Day was cut down: yet I did not heare that the party was punished'.

Following the restoration of the monarchy, cuttings from other Glastonbury thorns were used to replace the Wearyall Hill tree. In 1684 young Glastonbury thorn trees were changing hands at a crown each. As recorded on page 237, the move in 1752 to the new calendar re-invigorated interest in the Christmas flowering of the plant. The original Wearyall Hill tree was commemorated in 1800 when an inscribed stone was placed on the exact place where it had grown.

IN THE MIDDLE OF THE 17TH CENTURY, CROMWELL ROOTED OUT WHAT WAS CONSIDERED TO BE PAGAN OR PAPAL IDOLATRY. THE CUSTOM OF SENDING A SPRAY OF GLASTONBURY THORN TO THE MONARCH ABRUPTLY STOPPED.

In 1929 the custom of sending a pre-Christmas spray to the Royal Family was revived. Until its death in 1991, the new source was a tree in the churchyard of St John's Church, Glastonbury. Another Glastonbury tree now supplies the twigs. About a week before Christmas local school children sing carols while the vicar and mayor cut budded twigs that are sent to the Queen (and, until 2001, the Queen Mother). Since it featured on the Christmas stamp in 1986, there has been a revival of interest in the plant and stock is maintained by a number of specialist nurseries.

Whatever one's beliefs as to the origin of the Glastonbury tree it is certainly a biological oddity, now referred to scientifically as *Crataegus monogyna* – 'Biflora'. What are the facts, as distinct from the stories, about this plant? The first point is that it is not regarded as a separate species but as a cultivar (cultivated variety) of the common hawthorn. The features of the Glastonbury thorn are very similar to those of common hawthorn although the leaves are often slightly smaller than normal. Additionally, of course, there is the winter flush of new leaves and flowers (though unlike the May-time flowers, these do not set fruit).

Many of the earlier accounts of the tree made out that the winter flowers did not open until Christmas Eve (by the old calendar), some even stipulating midnight as the exact opening time. (This was widely believed to be the time of Christ's birth.) Even in those days it was suggested that the opening of the buds was accelerated by heat from lanterns held by the inquisitive crowd. An objective account of the thorn was provided by Philip Miller in his well-known *Gardeners Dictionary* (first published in 1735), when he commented that the opening on Christmas Day 'to a great measure depends on the Mildness of the Season'.

In *Flora Britannica*, Mabey records, 'These days the blossoming of the trees is extremely variable, sometimes, after a mild autumn, as early as November, sometimes not until early March if there is a severe winter.' The lack of Christmas flowering at the instigation of the new calendar pales into insignificance when set beside the influence of climate change. Shortly before Christmas 2000, I was delighted to share with the Queen the pleasure of receiving several flowering sprays of Glastonbury thorn. My present came from the Glastonbury garden of Pat and Robert Ayles, who informed me that their tree had started to flower at the end of September and had been in full bloom by early November.

There are winter-flowering forms of hawthorn in southern Europe that also have the smaller leaves of the Glastonbury thorn, but nowhere else in Europe or the Middle East is there a hawthorn with two distinct flowering periods. The scientific explanation is that the plant is an interesting sport (mutation), a claim backed by the recent discovery of a self-sown 'Biflora' tree in a Midlands nature reserve.

Long-established grafts from trees in Glastonbury are part of other local Christmas customs. These include the thorn at Appleton already mentioned, one at Shenley in Buckinghamshire and the Gilpin thorn at Houghton-le-Spring near Durham. Such Christmas hawthorn customs are specific to Britain, unlike the much more widespread Christmas tree tradition.

A Christmas Butterfly – the Holly Blue

There is only one species of British butterfly in which the caterpillars of two different broods eat different food plants at different seasons of the year, and this is the Holly Blue (*Celastrina argiolus*). The butterfly overwinters as short, fat hibernating pupae from which the adults emerge from late March onwards, when they can be seen flying around holly trees. The female (which unlike that of other British blues, is predominantly blue, not brown) lays her eggs among the flower buds of holly and these, together with the new leaves, provide food for the caterpillars prior to pupation from July onwards.

The second brood of adults emerges in July and August, but this time the females seek out the young flower buds of ivy as nourishment for their caterpillars. From September each caterpillar is transformed to a pupa – the stage that sees it through the winter. The spring brood eats holly flower buds and the autumn brood devours ivy flower buds, thus neatly exploiting the very different flowering seasons of these two well-known Christmas plants.

When I first arrived in Sheffield in 1978 the holly blue was an unusual sighting. Its distribution was then predominantly through the southern counties of England and Wales with far fewer records from more northern areas. It has, however become more common in Yorkshire over the past 20 years. While the human population of Britain continues to drift southward, the holly blue, possibly as a result of climate change, is going the other way.

Some colonies of the butterfly have developed a taste for different food. In parts of the west country both generations use gorse as a food plant. Another alternative food plant for the holly blue is the shrub known as snowberry (*Symphoricarpos rivularis*). This 19th-century introduction from North America is best known for its marble-sized, white berries that look like miniature snowballs. Like holly, ivy and mistletoe, the snowberry's fruits are present over the winter months and provide food for birds when little else is available.

The image of snowberry has recently appeared on Christmas cards but the plant is unlikely to challenge holly, mistletoe or ivy for a place in the Christmas decorations, not least because it drops its leaves in the autumn. All our traditional Christmas plants are evergreen or, as in the case of the Glastonbury thorn, produce fresh leaves at Christmas.

Unexpected Animals in the House

On the first page of this book I commented that many people believe that the Nativity scene, as portrayed in the Gospels, included a number of animals, especially the ox and the ass. In fact, no animals are mentioned, although Luke comes close in his passage about the shepherds 'keeping watch over their flock' and 'abiding in the field ... in the same country'. The shepherds had to travel to Bethlehem to see the 'babe lying in a manger' and in that they 'came with haste' it seems unlikely that their flocks (much more likely to have been goats rather than sheep) would have come with them.

Some authors have argued that the presence of livestock in the stable (or sharing the living room at night as explained on page 18) would have been too commonplace to bother mentioning in the Gospel accounts, and that the lack of a mention does not preclude them from the event. It is the 8th-century pseudo-Matthew apocryphal version of the Gospels that includes the ox and the ass adoring the infant Jesus. The account also explains that this fulfilled the prophecy made by Habakkuk: 'Between two animals you are made manifest.'

Since then the ox and ass have regularly featured in paintings of the Nativity and by the 11th century were even depicted standing in the manger along with the baby Jesus. Lowing cattle are also featured in carols such as 'Away in a Manger', while great paintings have furthered the image of animals at the scene, none more so than Rubens's *Adoration of the Magi* that shows camels (the supposed mode of transport for the Magi) looking in on the scene.

Just as the reindeer is remarkably well suited to life in the frozen north, so the camel is the great survivor in the deserts of Africa and Arabia. Its body thermostat allows the camel's temperature to rise by as much as 6°C above that of its surroundings. Other mammals keep cool by sweating, effective but resulting in much loss of water. The hump contains not water (a common misconception) but fatty tissue on which the animal can draw when food and water are in short supply. A camel can lose up to 25 per cent of its body weight (mostly from its hump) and still function normally. Wind-blown sand is kept from its eyes by very bristly eyebrows and a protective membrane. Similarly, the ears of camels are covered with long hairs to keep out sand particles. Long used as a beast of burden, it can carry up to half a tonne, so a wise man and his present would have posed no problems.

IN BRITAIN THE NATIVITY PLAY, SPOKEN IN LATIN, BEGAN IN CHURCH AS PART OF THE SERVICES IN DECEMBER BEFORE IT BECAME MORE POPULAR WHEN PERFORMED IN ENGLISH ON THE STREETS. FOLLOWING ITS SUPPRESSION BY THE PURITANS IN THE 17TH CENTURY, IT WAS NOT WIDELY RE-ENACTED UNTIL ITS REVIVAL BY INFANT AND PRIMARY SCHOOLS IN THE 20TH CENTURY.

It is, however, to 13th-century Italy and the antics of St Francis of Assisi on a hillside outside the town of Greccio that we owe the beginnings of the Nativity play where animals occupy some of the leading roles. In 1223 (three years before he died) St Francis staged the first Nativity play with a wooden manger (crib) full of hay, together with an ox and an ass. According to local legend the hay from the crib at Greccio was later used to cure sick animals and was even valued as a remedy against the plague.

In Britain the Nativity play, spoken in Latin, began in church as part of the services in December before it became more popular when performed in English on the streets. Following its suppression by the Puritans in the 17th century, it was not widely re-enacted until its revival by infant and primary schools in the 20th century. Many a proud parent or grandparent has since had to sit through a whole performance in order to catch a glimpse of their loved one playing the third angel or first donkey, or even appearing as a crocodile or Teletubby, both unlikely to have been present at the original Nativity. The donkey is present by virtue of its having been the most likely animal on which the pregnant Mary travelled to Bethlehem. Legend has it that it was a donkey that carried the cross prior to the crucifixion and the mark of the cross left the darker, cross-like pattern still found on the back of a donkey. The song 'Little Donkey' is now a staple of almost all school Nativity plays.

The crib (in the sense of a model of the Nativity) has evolved with the Nativity play, though it was not apparently part of the pre-Reformation Christmas in Britain. Even by 1900 cribs were confined to Roman Catholic and a few Anglican churches from where they have spread to most churches, together with infant schools and shop windows.

Animals also feature in the folklore of Christmas. The cock, closely associated with Christ's betrayal, is said to have been the first animal to announce the birth of Jesus when other animals are supposed to have started to talk. On Christmas Eve bees are said to hum the Hundredth Psalm in their hives, and at the start of Christmas Day cattle are thought to turn to the east and bow. Sadly for many animals Christmas Day is a less happy occasion as they form the basis of the feast long associated with the seasonal celebrations.

Dr Joel Poinsett and his Poisonous Plant

Having spent many of my formative infant years in Egypt, I arrived back in England in 1955 and began to participate in a more typically British Christmas. During my teenage years I helped with the decoration of the tree and the seemingly endless production of coloured paper chains. At this time the middle classes were being wooed by a new Christmas table decoration known as the winter cherry. This little evergreen plant produces starry, white flowers and masses of shiny, orange or red, cherry-like fruits. Unfortunately, *Solanum capsicastrum*, to give it its scientific name, is related to deadly nightshade and its attractive berries, though less toxic than the nightshade, cause severe sickness if ingested.

In the mid-1960s, as I left home to continue my studies at university, there were several contenders for the number one Christmas potted plant, including an old favourite. Poinsettia, also known as the Mexican flame leaf (*Euphorbia pulcherrima*), is a spreading, sparsely branched shrub that reaches a height of 4m in its native Mexico. In December the large leaves (scientifically termed involucral bracts) at the apex of each branch turn bright crimson and completely overshadow the tiny yellow flowers at their base.

The dominance of red as the Christmas colour has already been noted. From red-berried holly to red candles and red crackers and the much-loved robin, the British Christmas has a ruddy hue. In America red candles and crackers are no problem, but the wildlife is less accommodating. The American robin (*Turdus migratorius*), the one that goes 'Bob, bob, bobbing', is a chestnut-red-breasted member of the thrush family. It is far from the red-faced cheeky European robin. In searching for an alternative red symbol of Christmas, the citizens of the United States did not have to look far.

It was in the 1820s that Dr Joel Poinsett discovered the Mexican shrub and by 1829 he was exhibiting it at the Pennsylvania Horticultural Show where it aroused a great deal of interest. It rapidly caught on in those more western states where it could be grown outdoors. In the 1830s it was introduced to Britain, but as a subtropical shrub it could not survive outdoors and it grew too large to be easily accommodated indoors. By 1900 it was being grown commercially, as a pot plant, in both countries, but even as I set off for university in 1964, the art of growing short-stemmed, Christmas-flowering poinsettias was fraught with difficulties.

Most growers took cuttings and placed them under high-light conditions, up against the greenhouse glass. This produced neat plants but the red leaves were small and the method was expensive. In the late 1960s, Paul Ecke, a producer in California, began using a dwarfing hormone to keep the plants small. By combining this hormone with an eight-week regimen in the autumn when the plants were kept in complete darkness for at least 14 hours a day (flower production in poinsettias is triggered by short day-length), he produced short, well-branched plants with large coloured bracts in good time for Christmas.

By the 1990s his ranch was producing over 80 per cent of the world's poinsettias and for many the plant had ousted holly as the best-known Christmas plant. As with Christmas trees it later became fashionable not to have the common type. By the new millennium plant breeders had come up with more than 40 cultivars and these include plants with multiple whorls of 'leaves' and those with white, cream or purple 'leaves'. Many of these plants are now grown in Britain. Fashion has moved away from the original requirement of a red symbol.

It is perhaps ironic that the winter cherry with its poisonous berries has been usurped by poinsettia, which contains a sap capable of causing a severe skin rash. Given the poisonous nature of ivy and mistletoe we seem to be continuing a tradition of bringing poisonous plants into our houses as part of the Christmas decorations.

The Christmas poinsettia trade is now a multi-million-pound business, made more successful by the fact that few people manage to keep them alive and get them back in flower for the following Christmas. For those who like a challenge, be prepared to cut off the old flower heads and limit the watering until April. At this stage cut the plant back to about 10cm (4 inches) in height and move it to a warm place. Then it needs a minimum of 14 hours of autumnal darkness every 24 hours, after which there is at least a chance of a second colourful Christmas.

As with the robin there is a story that links poinsettia more closely to the Nativity story. In the plant's native Mexico it is known as 'the flower of the Holy Night' and legend has it that many years ago a poor peasant girl called Maria was visited by an angel. The angel asked the girl why she was crying and her reply was that she was too poor to buy a gift to take to the service on Christmas Eve. The angel told her to pick the tops from a nearby poinsettia bush. As Maria and her brother Pablo carried the plants into the church, everyone laughed at their green weeds, but when the upper leaves suddenly became a vivid scarlet star, the people fell to their knees and the children proudly made their offering at the crib.

Other best-selling potted plants for Christmas include the popular Christmas cactus. This fleshy leaved plant with its winter-flowering showy red or pink flowers is a garden hybrid between two species of *Schlumbergera* that grow in the Brazilian rainforest. New favourites at the start of the 21st century include the evergreen moth orchid (genus *Phalaenopsis*) of which there are many different hybrids, most remaining in bloom for many months (if not overwatered). Another is flaming katy (*Kalanchoe blossfeldiana*) with thick, glossy leaves and masses of small red, yellow or purple flowers. No doubt the lucrative trade in potted plants at Christmas will tempt us with new seasonal delights during the Christmases yet to come.

Stamp Shortages and the Second-class Tradition

In 1904 the King of Denmark lent his support to an idea developed by a postal clerk in Copenhagen. This was the production of Christmas seals to add to cards and parcels. The seals, at a penny each, raised money for the building of two hospitals dedicated to treating children with tuberculosis. Before the First World War the idea had spread to a number of other countries.

In many parts of the world, specially designed stamps are issued for Christmas, and the Post Office first issued British Christmas stamps in 1966. In 1986 the 13p stamp featured the Glastonbury thorn, the 18p one depicted three ladies partaking in the Welsh Plygain service, whilst the 34p stamp commemorated Hereford's Boy Bishop. In many years, stamps encompass a particular theme. In 1988 Bethlehem, the shepherds, three wise men and the Nativity scene comprised a more religious series. In 1995 the five special stamps all depicted a robin. The second-class design was of a robin sitting in the posting slot of a post box, so reinforcing the likely origin of the robin's place on our Christmas cards. In 1997, the stamps all featured a cracker, as it was then 150 years since the beginnings of our modern cracker.

The Guernsey Post Office has produced some very attractive Christmas stamps. In 1984 the 5p stamp appeared in 12 different versions with each one depicting a different image from the 'Twelve Days of Christmas' rhyme. In 1998, six Christmas stamps celebrated another 150th anniversary – the popularisation of the Christmas tree custom in Britain by Victoria and Albert. Images representing the 1930s and 1960s featured synthetic trees but the 1990s' picture was of a real one.

By 2001 the old Post Office had changed its name to Consignia and the second-class Christmas stamp featured two robins wrapping a scarf around the neck of a snowman. Some 315 million of these stamps were printed but this was exceeded by the 360 million first-class Christmas stamps. Despite a campaign to persuade people to use first-class stamps, it was supplies of the muffled snowman that began to run out just before Christmas. One sub-postmaster commented, 'Everyone buys second-class stamps for Christmas. It's tradition.' Consignia's management may have believed that they could overcome this tradition but the great British public proved otherwise.

The Post Office monopoly on the delivery of letters was relaxed some years ago to permit charities to benefit from any profit made delivering Christmas cards. In 1981 a venture scout group in Woodseats (in south Sheffield) started a local delivery with specially designed and printed stamps. In the run-up to Christmas, stamped cards were collected from local shops, sorted and delivered, by the scouts and their parents. The Scout post (the first of its kind in the country) quickly spread to the rest of Sheffield and parts of north Derbyshire, and in 1985 almost a million Sheffield Scout stamps (five designs at 10p) were printed.

This alternative service ceased after deliveries in the year 2000, but over 20 years it raised some £150,000 for charities and also valuable funds for local scout groups. For the first three years the stamps were printed in just one colour but the more recent ones were produced in four colours. Collectors from all over the world have sought the remaining stamps, currently available from Roger Sanderson on 0114 2301835.

Music, the Big Screen and the Queen

Perhaps the work of classical music most often associated with Christmas is *Messiah*. This Christmas oratorio composed by Handel was first performed in Dublin in 1742 where, in the spirit of the season, it benefited a number of Irish charities. If *Messiah* is the most popular Christmas work for choir and orchestra then the best-known ballet of the season is Tchaikovsky's *The Nutcracker*.

Popular music has long used Christmas as a theme, if sometimes rather indirectly. One of the most often performed pieces of Christmas music was composed as long ago as 1857 when it was entitled 'One Horse Open Sleigh' by its composer James Pierpont. What we now know as 'Jingle Bells' was actually written for the American Thanksgiving celebration. With the popularisation of the sleigh-riding St Nicholas figure accompanying Nast's illustrations to Clement Moore's poem, so 'Jingle Bells' moved over to become a Christmas favourite.

Irving Berlin's song 'White Christmas' was sung by Bing Crosby in the 1954 film of the same name, but Crosby had also performed it in an earlier film. This was *Holiday Inn*, which was released in 1942, the same year that Berlin won an Oscar for the song. Over the 60 years since then, not only has the song been the most played of all Christmas songs but it has made more money than any other popular song.

The 1940s also witnessed the gestation of what was to become another Christmas favourite. Taken from a 1942 short story written by Robert May, Johny Marks composed 'Rudolph the Red-nosed Reindeer' in 1949. After 50 years Rudolph is now much more famous than Dasher, Prancer and co., the eight reindeer mentioned in Moore's poem. The present-giver himself features in 'Santa Claus is Coming to Town', a song written in 1934 and one that has been recorded by many artists including Bing Crosby, Frank Sinatra, Bruce Springsteen and the Jackson 5.

The 1950s gave us Harry Belafonte and 'Mary's Boy Child', an unusual hit in that it was more like a carol and, unlike most Christmas songs, it concentrated on the religious aspect of Christmas. Another success was 'Little Donkey', a hit for such diverse artistes as Gracie Fields, The Beverley Sisters, and Nina and Frederick. The 1950s also came up with 'The Little Boy That Santa Forgot', as sung by Nat 'King' Cole. In 1956 the Goons released 'I'm Walking Backwards for Christmas' which reached number four in the charts.

By the 1960s a successful Christmas song, or any number one single at Christmas time, was a guarantee of financial success. Top forty hits of the decade included Brenda Lee's 'Rockin' Around the Christmas Tree', Dora Bryan with 'All I Want For Christmas is a Beatle' and 'Run Rudolph Run' by Chuck Berry.

More recent Christmas hits have included Slade's 'Merry Xmas Everybody', which after nearly 30 years is still widely played as part of the muzak in shops during the run-up to Christmas. Of a similar vintage are Wizzard's 'I Wish it Could be Christmas Every Day' and Michael Jackson's revival of 'Rockin' Robin'. During the 1980s the theme of charity returned to the festive season with Band Aid's chart-topping 'Do They Know it's Christmas' (1984) that boosted relief for Ethiopia.

Other highflyers have included 'Walking in the Air', sung by Aled Jones, from the Raymond Briggs animated film *The Snowman*. The top spot for Christmas 1999 saw a return to a more religious theme as Sir Cliff Richard sang the words of the Lord's Prayer to the tune of 'Auld Lang Syne'. His 'Millennium Prayer' received useful publicity when Radio 1 refused to play it.

Into the new millennium and the Christmas number one still sells more copies than hits at other times of the year. In 2000 the Christmas slot was held by 'Can We Fix It?' by Bob The Builder. This television spin-off sold 200,000 more copies than any other number one during that year.

DURING THE FINAL TWO DECADES OF THE 20TH CENTURY, VIEWING FIGURES INDICATED THAT ON SOME CHRISTMAS DAYS MORE THAN 70 PER CENT OF THE POPULATION WAS WATCHING TELEVISION IN THE PEAK EVENING SLOT – A FAR CRY FROM THE PARLOUR GAMES AND CHARADES OF EARLIER GENERATIONS.

Films with a Christmas theme, or just family films released for the Christmas holidays, have become a part of Christmas and in particular the festive television schedules. Two early Christmas films have already been mentioned with reference to the music they included, namely *Holiday Inn* (1942) and *White Christmas* (1954). Bing Crosby starred in both, with Fred Astaire and Danny Kaye respectively. *A Christmas Carol* (Dickens) has provided the storyline for many Christmas films, including *The Muppets' Christmas Carol*.

Other Christmas films include *Santa Claus – The Movie* with Dudley Moore and the recent success of *The Grinch*, where the hero hates Christmas. Cartoons with a Christmas theme include *Father Christmas* and *The Snowman*, both based on the books by Raymond Briggs and for many years a feature of the Christmas television schedules.

While for years the Christmas evening showing of the *Morecombe and Wise Show* was the most watched television at Christmas this later gave way to films, including the James Bond movies and other so-called family films. During the final two decades of the 20th century, viewing figures indicated that on some Christmas Days more than 70 per cent of the population was watching television in the peak evening slot – a far cry from the parlour games and charades of earlier generations. By the start of the 21st century the lure of computer games, and the popularity of videos, resulted in lower peak-viewing figures, with soaps such as *EastEnders* and *Coronation Street* among the most watched shows.

Radio was the medium used in 1932 for the first of what was to become another Christmas custom – the Christmas Day broadcast by the reigning monarch. This was initiated by John (later Lord) Reith in the year that the BBC received its royal charter. George V's speech was relayed from Sandringham and the words, written by Rudyard Kipling, began 'I speak now from my home and from my heart, to you all ...'

A further three Christmas broadcasts followed before the death of George V in 1936. There was a break of three years after George VI came to the throne. George, who stammered and had been unwilling to continue with the broadcasts, was persuaded to boost the war effort with a Christmas message in 1939. Following this he delivered an annual broadcast until the year of his death.

Queen Elizabeth II has continued the broadcasts through an era when more people watched her on television than listened to her on the radio. The theme of the family and the family of nations (now the Commonwealth) has been a common thread in most of the broadcasts. The 3pm slot was chosen for the first broadcast so as to ensure a maximum audience not only in Britain but also in the rest of the Empire.

In the early 1960s over 70 per cent of the population either watched or listened to the speech. In 1963 the broadcast was moved to 9.30am and the audience figures plummeted. The following year the 3pm slot was reinstated but the 1960 figures were never regained and in 1969 the message was dropped from the broadcasting schedules. Protests led to its reinstatement in 1970, but the audience figures had dropped below 50 per cent by the end of the 1980s. In the early 1990s the viewing audience was some 20 million; this dropped to just over 10 million in 2000 and 8.7 million in 2001. One way in which future audience figures may be boosted is the proposal to convert the message to a shortened text message and send it to mobile phones: 'BW 2 u all HMQE2'.

Why a White Christmas?

Why do people dream of a white Christmas? Long before the birth of Christ, snow would have been a frequent guest at the pagan midwinter Yuletide celebrations of northern Europe. Snow is, however, an uncommon sight in Bethlehem, so why is it that a 'traditional' Christmas conjures up pictures of shepherds keeping watch over their flocks in the snow? The 'White Christmas' song originated in America, where winter snowfalls in the east-coast states are all too common, but white Christmases in most areas of Britain are the exception rather than the rule. On the Isles of Scilly snow falls on only two days a year on average, while in central London the figure rises to twelve, and Edinburgh twenty. For many parts of Britain the number of days when snow covers the ground is also small: only three in central London, nine in Manchester and fifteen in Edinburgh.

Snow cover at Christmas is obviously a more common event in north-east Scotland than it is in London, where the chance of even a few flakes falling on Christmas Day is fewer than one in twelve. On only two occasions in the last century, 1938 and 1981, was there a white Christmas covering more than 50 per cent of Britain. Winter snow cover is, however, like the rest of our weather, very variable from year to year and in severe winters (1946/47, 1962/63 and 1978/79) many areas of Britain experienced more than 50 days of snow cover, though not necessarily at Christmas.

It was the severe winters of the 19th century that gave rise to our love affair with the white Christmas. Between 1812 and 1825 there were no fewer than six cold, snowy winters that even affected the south of England. These winters left a lasting impression on the young Charles Dickens, born in 1812. A run of warmer winters was reversed in the 1830s and the 1830/31 winter was an especially cold and snowy one. In 1836 and early 1837, not long after this severe winter, Dickens' first novel (originally entitled *The Posthumous Papers of the Pickwick Club*) was issued in 12 monthly parts. After 1837 when it was published as a book (entitled *The Pickwick Papers*) it became a huge success and the snowy Christmas at Dingley Dell quickly became a part of the Victorian idealised Christmas.

> 'Well, Sam,' said Mr Pickwick, as that favoured servitor entered his bedchamber with his warm water on the morning of Christmas Day. 'Still frosty?'
> 'Water in the wash-hand basin's a mask o' ice, sir,' responded Sam.
> 'Severe weather, Sam,' observed Mr Pickwick.
> 'Fine time for them as is well wropped up, as the polar bear said to himself ven he was practising his skating,' replied Mr Weller.
> Old Wardle led the way to a pretty large sheet of ice; and the fat boy and Mr Weller having shovelled and swept away the snow which had fallen on it during the night, Mr Bob Sawyer adjusted his skates …

In 1836, as the Pickwick story was being serialised, there was a very heavy snowfall that held up the mail, which in those days was moved by stagecoach. Dickens was to explore the Christmas theme in much greater detail in his Christmas books, the first and most well-known, *A Christmas Carol*, appearing in 1843. Once again

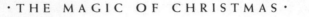

the cold, snowy weather is a feature of the Christmas being described. This was also when the commercial Christmas card was emerging so it is little wonder that favourite pictures included snowy scenes (often with stagecoaches) and skating figures – images that have remained on cards ever since.

The 1860s also saw the importation of the Americanised Santa Claus to Britain, complete with his associated snowy images, sleigh rides, jingling bells and reindeer (a mixture of north European and American east-coast winter scenes). Santa's snowy footprints as he made his way from the fireplace helped to fortify the belief that a perfect Christmas required some of the white stuff.

Children's books have also promoted the image that the ideal Christmas is a white one. Snowballs and more especially snowmen have also been caught up in the Christmas story. Raymond Briggs' *The Snowman* has become as much a part of Christmas on television as the Queen's speech. References to snowmen go back at least 500 years and in several countries, such as in 19th-century America, they represented symbols of authority that were attacked and destroyed by the young or underprivileged.

It is only in more recent times that the snowman has become a secular icon of Christmas. Despite recent revelations that the typical snowman is racist (always white), sexist and a reminder of masculine dominance outside the home, carrots are still used to portray noses rather than more intimate body parts. Fortunately for most of us he remains a figure of fun and a good excuse to venture outdoors and burn off some of the calories resulting from too much food and too little exercise over Christmas.

The Shape of Christmases to Come

This book has investigated the myths and magic of Christmas in its many guises. I hope that readers will have learnt something new and will now have a greater understanding of what has become an international celebration in honour of an event that took place in Bethlehem over 2,000 years ago.

A theme of the book has been to show how Christmas has subsumed earlier customs and changed with the times. The midwinter season has always been a time for foretelling the future, so what of the future of Christmas? Will the festival become ever more secular or will there be a return to the religious significance of the Nativity? How will new technology continue to impact on the traditions of Christmas?

What new foods will become fashionable? And will plum puddings and sprouts become as outmoded as frumenty and lambswool?

I am tempted to predict that, with the impact of climate change, Britain will continue to experience warmer winters, with less ice and snow to provide a white Christmas. Alternatively, if the change results in the shutting off of the Gulf Stream, future Christmas weather may indeed be deep and crisp and even colder.

BIBLIOGRAPHY

Auden, W. H., *Collected Poems* Faber and Faber (1976)

Baker, Margaret, *Discovering Christmas Customs and Folklore* (1968) Shire Publications Ltd

Briggs, J., *Kissing Goodbye to Mistletoe* (1999) Plantlife

Carroll, Lewis, *Alice's Adventures in Wonderland* (1865) Macmillan

Cooke, Mordecei, *A Plain and Easy Account of British Fungi* (1862) S.P.C.K.

Count, E. W. and Count, A. L., *4000 Years of Christmas* (1997) Ulysses Press

Davies, Norman, *The Isles* (1999) Macmillan

Dawson, W. F., *Christmas and its Associations* (1902) Elliot Stock

Dickens, Charles, *A Christmas Carol* (1843) Chapman and Hall

–, *Hard Times* (1854) Chapman and Hall

–, *The Pickwick Papers* (1836–7) Chapman and Hall

Duncan, David, *The Calendar* (1998) Fourth Estate

Frazer, J. G., *The Golden Bough* (1922) Macmillan

Golby, J.M. and Purdue, A. W., *The Making of the Modern Christmas* (1986) B.T. Batsford.

Harding, Patrick, Lyon, Tony and Tomblin, Gill, *How to Identify Edible Mushrooms* (1996) HarperCollins

Hardy, T., *Under the Greenwood Tree* (1872)

Higgs, Michelle, *Christmas Cards* (1999) Shire Publications Ltd

Highfield, Roger, *Can Reindeer Fly? The Science of Christmas* (1998) Metro

Innes-Smith, R., *A Derbyshire Christmas* (1992) Alan Sutton

Irving, Washington, *Knickerbocker's History of New York* (1809)

Lack, David, *The Life of the Robin* (1943) H. F. & G. Witherby Ltd

Lee, Laurie, *Cider with Rosie* (1959) Chatto & Windus

Mabey, Richard (ed), *Flora Britannica* (1996) Sinclair Stevenson

Miller, Daniel (ed), *Unwrapping Christmas* (1995) Clarendon Press

Muldoon, Paul, *Why Brownlie Left* Faber and Faber (1980)

Thiede, C. P. and D'Ancona M., *The Quest for the True Cross* (2000) Weidenfeld & Nicolson

Tolkien, J. R. R., *The Father Christmas Letters* (1976) George Allen & Unwin

Van Renterghen, Tony, *When Santa was a Shaman* (1995) Llewellyn

Various, *Holy Bible* (King James Version) (1611)

Warner, Susan, *The Christmas Stocking* (1854)

Waugh, Evelyn, *Brideshead Revisited* (1945)

CREDITS

Grateful acknowledgement is made to the following for permission to reproduce extracts used in this book:

Extract from *Cider With Rosie* by Laurie Lee, originally published by the Hogarth Press. Reproduced by permission of The Random House Group Ltd.

Extract from a letter to David Lack from Richard Meinertzhagen, reproduced by permission of *British Wildlife* magazine (Lack, P 2001 *British Wildlife* 13: 95-100)

Lines from ' For the Time Being: A Christmas Oratorio' from *The Collected Poems* by W.H. Auden reproduced by permission of Faber and Faber UK and also by Edward Mendelson, William Meredith and Monroe K. Spears, Executors of the Estate of W.H. Auden, used by permission of Random House Inc, New York

Grateful acknowledgement is made to the following for permission to reproduce extracts used in this book:

Extract from *Cider With Rosie* by Laurie Lee, originally published by the Hogarth Press. Reproduced by permission of The Random House Group Ltd.

Extract from a letter to David Lack from Richard Meinertzhagen, reproduced by permission of *British Wildlife* magazine (Lack, P 2001 *British Wildlife* 13: 95-100)

Lines from ' For the Time Being: A Christmas Oratorio' from *The Collected Poems* by W.H. Auden reproduced by permission of Faber and Faber UK and also by Edward Mendelson, William Meredith and Monroe K. Spears, Executors of the Estate of W.H. Auden, used by permission of Random House Inc, New York
ı
Truce' by Paul Muldoon from *Why Brownlie Left* reproduced by permission of Faber and Faber UK and from *Poems: 1968-1998* reproduced by permission of Farrar, Strauss and Giroux, LLC, USA

INDEX